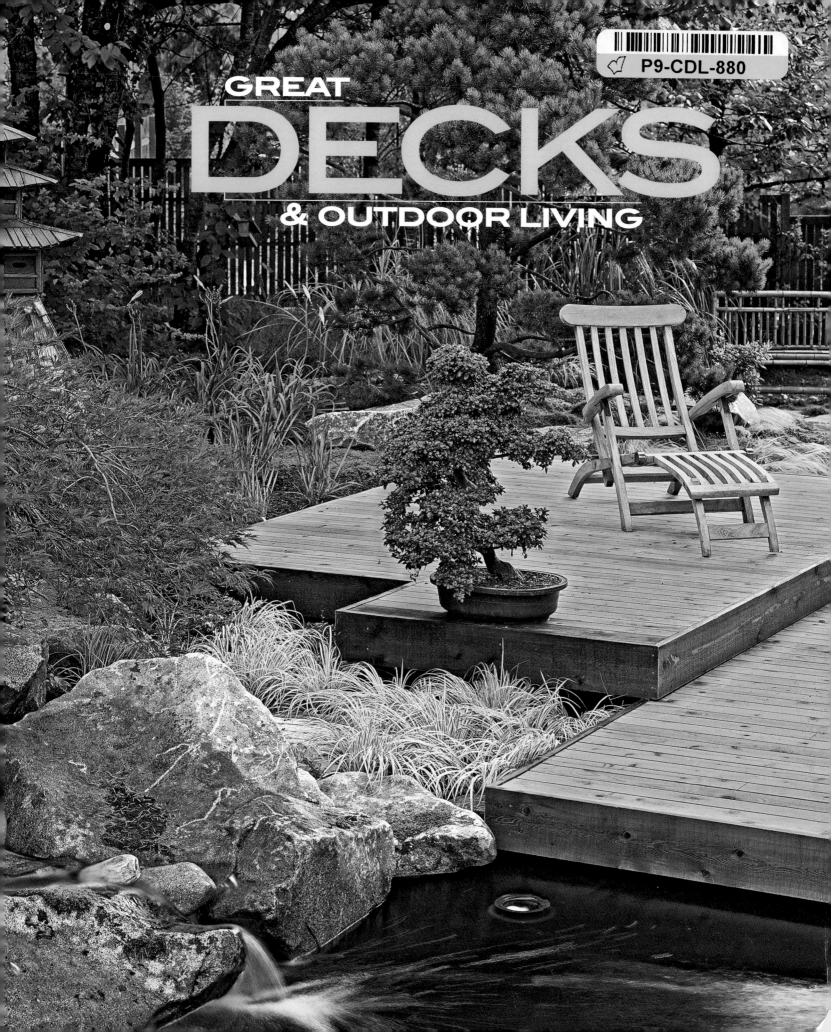

GREAT
DECKS
& OUTDOOR LIVING

Great Decks & Outdoor Living
Editors: Vicki Christian, Paula Marshall
Project Manager: Catherine M. Staub, Lexicon Consulting, Inc.
Contributing Editor: Julie Collins, Lexicon Consulting, Inc.
Contributing Writers: Dan Nelson, Kelly Roberson, Andrea Schmidt, Lexicon Consulting, Inc.
Graphic Designer: David Jordan, Studio 22
Copy Chief: Terri Fredrickson
Publishing Operations Manager: Karen Schirm
Senior Editor, Asset and Information Manager: Phillip Morgan
Edit and Design Production Coordinator: Mary Lee Gavin
Editorial Assistant: Kaye Chabot
Book Production Managers: Pam Kvitne, Marjorie J. Schenkelberg, Rick von Holdt, Mark Weaver
Contributing Copy Editor and Indexer: Don Gulbrandsen
Contributing Proofreaders: Dan Degan, Sherry Hames, Sara Henderson
Cover Photographer: Stephen Cridland

Meredith® Books
Executive Director, Editorial: Gregory H. Kayko
Executive Director, Design: Matt Strelecki
Managing Editor: Amy Tincher-Durik
Executive Editor/Group Manager: Denise L. Caringer
Marketing Product Manager: Tyler Woods

Publisher and Editor in Chief: James D. Blume
Editorial Director: Linda Raglan Cunningham
Executive Director, New Business Development: Todd M. Davis
Executive Director, Sales: Ken Zagor
Director, Operations: George A. Susral
Director, Production: Douglas M. Johnston
Director, Marketing: Amy Nichols
Business Director: Jim Leonard

Vice President and General Manager: Douglas J. Guendel

Meredith Publishing Group
President: Jack Griffin
Executive Vice President: Bob Mate

Meredith Corporation
Chairman and Chief Executive Officer: William T. Kerr
President and Chief Operating Officer: Stephen M. Lacy

In Memoriam: E.T. Meredith III (1933-2003)

All of us at Meredith® Books are dedicated to providing you with information and ideas to enhance your home.
We welcome your comments and suggestions. Write to us at: Meredith Books, Home Decorating and Design
Editorial Department, 1716 Locust St., Des Moines, IA 50309-3023.

GREAT
DECKS
& OUTDOOR LIVING

GREAT DECKS
& OUTDOOR LIVING

CHAPTER THREE:
PATIOS, POOLS, AND COURTYARDS

GREAT
DECKS
& OUTDOOR LIVING

1 GRAND SPACES

Take a visual tour of stunning outdoor spaces to find inspiration for your own backyard. The ultimate outdoor escapes go beyond the basic deck or patio and encompass an entire living experience. Inviting retreats feature inspiring design, lush landscaping, and comfortable furnishings. Outdoor "rooms" provide a specialized environment for every activity. Whether you want to share an intimate alfresco meal with family or are looking to throw lavish dinner parties outdoors, a plethora of dining, cooking, and entertaining options ensure not even meal time will keep you away from the backyard. Seamlessly blend spas, pools, and outdoor fireplaces into your design to further expand your options. Don't forget thoughtful amenities such as gazebos, overheads, and screens—they're the key to ensuring your escape is private and protected.

Smooth Entertainer

Ambitious entertainers know a standard deck won't ever be the life of the party—especially if it's falling apart. Build level-upon-level of spaces for grilling, sitting by a fire, and swimming, however, and you're looking at a deck that's party-perfect.

Such is the case with Wayne and Fran Kirkpatrick's backyard escape. When their standard 18-foot deck—which didn't match the scale of the house and didn't span the back—began showing signs of age, Wayne knew the structure wasn't going to cut it.

"We like to entertain," Wayne says. "Fourth of July, New Year's Eve, baby showers—any excuse to cook out." But their love for entertaining was hindered by the too-small deck with the wood bowing and nails popping out.

EVEN THOUGH IT REQUIRED EXTRA SUPPORT UNDERNEATH, WAYNE CHOSE THIS EYE-CATCHING DIAMOND DECKING PATTERN.

MATCHING STAIRCASES RUN DOWN EACH SIDE OF THE SPRAWLING DECK, LEADING FROM THE SECOND STORY TO GROUND LEVEL.

INDOOR/OUTDOOR SPA LINKING DECK AND HOUSE

BUILT-IN BENCHES AROUND STONE FIRE PIT

INSET DIAMOND-PATTERN DECKING FOR VISUAL INTEREST

THE GROUND-LEVEL SPA FEATURES NATURAL WATER-FALLS AND JETS STRATEGICALLY PLACED NEAR SEATING LEDGES.

THE UPPER LEVEL HAS PLENTY OF ROOM FOR ENTERTAINING. WHEN THINGS HEAT UP, COPPER MISTERS ON THE WALL OF THE HOUSE COOL GUESTS.

WAYNE DESIGNED THE LIGHTING ON THE STAIRWAY RISERS. THOUGH SIMPLE, IT CREATES A PLEASING NIGHTTIME EFFECT.

Once the decision was made to replace the structure, Wayne's vision took hold and there was no stopping him. The new 40-foot-long deck he dreamed up required one month of planning and 10 months of construction, and it didn't come cheap.

To the Kirkpatrick family, it was worth it. The new multilevel structure features a step-down, octagon-shape seating area with drop-front storage benches, and a fire pit for roasting marshmallows; a spa that runs underground from outside to a screened-in room beneath the deck; and plenty of space for grilling, mingling, partying, or relaxing.

Although Wayne—who majored in landscape architecture in college, though he never pursued a career in it—envisioned much of the deck himself, he hired a designer to make the architectural drawings. With local builder Richard Kapuga, Wayne staked off the deck, only to realize it was much too small. Immediately they pushed the deck out another seven feet and tossed away the plans. "We did a lot of winging it," Wayne says. "One of us would say, 'Hey, wouldn't it be great if…,' and those are dangerous words."

Case in point: the decking pattern Wayne chose. Instead of a conventional floor, Wayne wanted a bull's-eye pattern like one he had seen at a hotel in England. This proved to be a challenge—Kapuga had to specially position boards to support the pattern because of the screened-in room beneath the deck. This resulted in a deeper-than-anticipated floor, which was disguised by adding a herringbone detail to the edge.

wall was useless visually otherwise," Wayne says. "Plus, I like the soothing effect of water."

As much as the finished deck provides entertaining space for Wayne, Fran, and their friends, the couple also considered how the structure could be used in the future. "We planned the deck with the kids in mind," Wayne says. "As they get older, we want a place where they want to hang out and bring their friends."

Another particularly ambitious moment came when Wayne wanted to add a water element to the design. He decided on a pond with koi, but Fran put her foot down. "Fran wanted something she could get into," Wayne says. "She yelled 'Spa!'"

Naturally, Wayne took the design well beyond the basics, and the result is an enchanting spa area that sits half inside the house and half outside, complete with programmable fiber-optic lighting. The wall separating the screened-patio portion from the outdoor spa area has a gap that allows users to duck underneath for movement between areas without getting out of the water. Inside the screened room, a waterfall cascades down a rock wall beside the spa, furthering the poolside ambience. "The

BUILT-IN BENCHES AROUND A FIRE PIT OFFER THE PERFECT SPOT FOR RELAXING DAY OR NIGHT.

A GASLIGHT CASTS A SOFT GLOW OVER THE SPA, WHICH REQUIRES SEVEN PUMPS: THREE FOR WATER-FALLS, TWO FOR WATER JETS, ONE FOR HEATING, AND ONE FOR RECIRCULATING WATER.

SOLID 4x4 POSTS COMBINE WITH STURDY WROUGHT-IRON RAILINGS TO COMPLEMENT THE 50 TONS OF BOULDERS THAT COMPRISE A NATURAL SURROUND FOR THE SPA.

REBEL WITH A CAUSE

Fresh from architecture school at Tulane University, Pete Conry realized that the predictable, builder-supplied deck on his parents' home near Des Moines, Iowa, was anything but an example of good design. Armed with his degree and helped by his friend, former boss, and carpenter Brian Moylan, Pete replaced the old, teetering structure with an elegant, spacious outdoor haven for parents Kenneth and Mary. It's a space that his mother calls "the nicest deck in Des Moines."

"Most people are happy with a rectangular deck. That's fine, but a deck can really be a special place," Pete says.

Without a particular house style to dictate his design choices, Pete turned for inspiration to a channel behind the home that connects a small lake with an overflow basin. When at capacity, lake water flows down stone steps through the channel and under a stone bridge. Pete envisioned a structure that would "merge the yard with the deck, which would flow out from the house," he says.

THREE DISTINCT LEVELS COMPRISE THE DECK: ON THE TOP LEVEL IS A HOT TUB, JUST TWO STEPS DOWN IS A DINING AREA, AND FURTHER DOWN IS A PATIO.

RAILINGS PROVIDE THE CONRYS WITH MORE PLACES TO SUSPEND HANGING FLOWER BOXES.

The new deck sweeps down from the house with two seating areas, a space for a hot tub, and a sweeping curved staircase that links the upper levels with a lower flagstone patio. The cascading design mimics the stonework, with "a stratified look, like stones moving under each other in a slate deposit," Pete says.

While wood is used for the bulk of the decking material, Pete chose custom-made steel railings, which are stronger than wood, lighter in appearance, and nearly maintenance-free once painted. The railings support three triangular planter boxes that jut out at sharp points, punctuating the view down the stairs. They also move the garden up into the deck, giving Mary, an avid gardener, more places to plant.

The planters sit atop translucent panels, which appear intermittently, cleverly disguising nighttime lanterns that evoke the windows of the house. Pete and Brian experimented with the right level of lighting, roughing up one side of the clear acrylic plastic panels with an orbital sander. The end result diffuses the light, allowing it to shine through while giving the panels an interesting texture. "I wanted the deck to come alive at night, and not just with standard deck lighting tricks," Pete says. "I wanted something that would look engaging and different, that would stand out but not look too garish."

The sweeping stairs, most with their own footings, each took a full day to assemble, but are critical to the design. They encourage traffic flow through the house

The sweeping lines of the staircase echo the cascading river rock behind the Conry's home.

Translucent panels punctuate the metal railing, while the angles of the deck are softened by the curves of the staircase.

A dining area on the middle level, separate from the uppermost portion of the deck, adds yet another spot for entertaining.

The steps that flow to the patio resemble a series of landings of varying shapes and sizes.

Custom-made steel railings contribute to the unique appearance of the deck. Once painted, the material is nearly maintenance-free.

The sharp points of the light boxes jut out into the space around the deck.

Even the smallest corners of the deck are home to plantings.

and down to each outdoor space, but are destinations themselves due to their depth and breadth. They provide spots to pause, chat, relax, or simply gaze at the garden.

The Conrys entertain often, and now have space for not only friends, but also their six children and their families. The deck and patio supply a unified area for dining without walls to enjoy the outdoors. Family and friends—grandchildren running to play or adults engaged in conversation—move easily between levels. "The old deck didn't engage the patio at all. There wasn't a link between people on the deck upstairs, coming out of the kitchen, and people coming out of the family room onto the patio," Pete says. "I thought it was important to merge the deck and the patio together."

While his parents provided an interesting test case for an architect-rebel in the making, the lessons learned are universal. "A deck serves as an additional and valuable room of the house, one that can be added at a relatively modest cost. It makes sense to sit down with an architect or a carpenter to come up with a design that suits your needs and expresses your personality," Pete says.

A MOVEABLE FIRE PIT ON THE STONE PATIO PROVIDES A WELCOME BURST OF WARMTH ON CHILLY NIGHTS.

DISTINCTIVE ILLUMINATION COMES FROM STAIR SPOTLIGHTS AND LIGHTING FROM BEHIND THE TRANSLUCENT PLASTIC PANELS.

LUXURY LEVELS

The northwest view out the back windows of Tom and Pam Faludy's suburban Denver home looks onto the stunning Front Range of the Rocky Mountains, so it seemed only natural for the couple to create an outdoor living space to take advantage of the scenery. They began with a plain-Jane rectangular redwood deck behind the home. That gradually evolved, first with the addition of a gazebo, then a kitchen, and finally a spa, each blending with the next for an appealing 2,000-square-foot outdoor living retreat.

Custom designer Steve Sparhawk drew inspiration for the gazebo from the angles of the home's bay windows overlooking the deck. The gazebo perches on wooden beams, adding a multidimensional layer to the space.

Two months before their oldest daughter's wedding and with 35 out-of-town guests on the way, Tom and Pam decided it was perfect timing for a third, and final, expansion. "We talked about expanding the deck for a long time," Pam says. "We wanted to provide more of an outdoor entertainment area that could be enjoyed by everyone."

Sparhawk added an outdoor cooking center, complete with a gas grill with a separate side burner and a small refrigerator. At the opposite end of the space from the gazebo is an 8×16-foot swim spa—a therapeutic spa big enough for the kids and their friends to use as a swimming pool.

The spa is built on a concrete slab foundation, with a redwood surround that gives it the look of a recessed pool. "I wanted the spa to look built-in—rather than stick out—so it would blend with the ambience of the entire backyard," Tom says.

THE ELEVATED GAZEBO GAZES ONTO A VIEW OF BIRCH, BLUE SPRUCE, AND ASPEN TREES, WITH THE ROCKY MOUNTAINS IN THE DISTANCE. STEPS LEAD TO VARIOUS LEVELS ON THE 2,000-FOOT SPACE.

To unify each addition, Sparhawk needed a transition zone between the original deck, gazebo, and spa area. He removed an old staircase that led to the backyard, and instead built a series of shorter, wider staircases that lead from the gazebo to the spa deck to ground level. Cedar replaced existing deck railings, and balusters and routed caps give the space a light, finished profile.

During the project, the couple realized the deck might block light to the ground-floor windows below the deck, so Sparhawk set the structure out several feet. A loggia just outside the walk-out basement, complete with built-in benches, allows the sun to filter in. It serves as a covered deck for lounging, adding yet another layer to the family's outdoor living zones.

The generous expanse of space maximizes the time the family of six spends outside, whether relaxing, dining, or entertaining. It's the perfect spot, with a perfect view.

THE GAZEBO, JUST OFF THE HOME'S ORIGINAL DECK, IS THE PERFECT SPOT FOR AN AFTERNOON MEAL. POTTED PLANTS INFUSE THE SPACE WITH COLOR.

TOM AND PAM FALUDY RELAX ON ONE OF THE DECK'S MANY LOUNGING AREAS.

A GAS GRILL AND OUTDOOR REFRIGERATOR MAKE
SUMMER COOKING A SNAP.

UNDERNEATH THE DECK, A LOGGIA COMES COMPLETE
WITH BENCHES FOR STORAGE AND A HAMMOCK; THE
VIEW LOOKS TOWARD A WATERFALL.

THE SPA DOUBLES AS A SWIMMING POOL. LOCATED
JUST STEPS FROM THE OUTDOOR KITCHEN, IT
WAS PART OF THE THIRD DECK PROJECT. A WOOD
SURROUND GIVES THE SPA A BUILT-IN FEEL, WHILE
STEPS SERVE AS A TRANSITION ZONE TO THE ORIGINAL
DECK AND THE GAZEBO.

MULTIPLE LEVELS FOR SEPARATE DINING SPACES

SUNKEN PATIO FOR ADDITIONAL SEATING

HANDCRAFTED ELEMENTS TO MATCH HOME'S DESIGN

MEANDERING PATHS TO CONNECT GARDEN ROOMS

At first glance, the 6-foot drop from house to property line in Donna and Chris Brightman's backyard might have intimidated lesser folks. But the couple, who had already transformed their dilapidated 1898 Victorian farmhouse into a comfortable home, welcomed the makeover, confident they could create a comfortable outdoor area that maximized living spaces.

Today, the once-overgrown yard is full of secluded and graceful spots, including a multilevel deck, patio, and courtyard, as well as ample areas for Donna to exercise her green thumb and for the couple's three children to play. "We spend every possible minute outside," Donna says . "It's important to us that we can live outdoors easily and comfortably."

CUSTOM-CRAFTED RAILINGS AND COLUMNS INTEGRATE THE DECK WITH THE HOME'S ARCHITECTURE. A LATTICE PROVIDES A SPOT FOR FRAGRANT BLOOMS TO CLIMB.

FROM THE TOP LEVEL, ADULTS CAN WATCH OVER KIDS EATING OR ROMPING ON THE PLAY SET, WHICH IS SCREENED BY A ROW OF HEDGES.

Before they jumped into construction, Donna and Chris spent time in their yard, looking at the house and sketching ideas for a deck. They were adamant that the eventual design preserve their home's historical integrity, and also wanted to screen views from the neighbors and a church next door. Builder Jim Ebbole took their pencil scratches and transformed them into a space that starts out flush with the house, perched above the fence line, quickly steps down to a seating area, then dips one last time to a secluded patio. A play set nestles at the back of the yard, screened by arborvitae and shrub roses.

Critical to the space's success are separate eating spaces: children dine on the lower level, under the watchful eye of parents on the upper deck. The grill, too, is above the main dining area and outside an entrance to the house, so guests and family can visit without the bother of smoke, yet the chef doesn't feel isolated. Large market umbrellas above the dining table enable family and friends to enjoy eating and relaxing even in hot Mid-west summers. "The lower deck sits just outside the sunroom and catches plenty of sun," Donna says. "But it's so open and airy that you can always catch a breeze there. We eat out there all the time, and it's the public space we use for entertaining."

Good, old-fashioned hand construction integrates the new deck with the vintage farmhouse, including custom-crafted, one-inch lattice panels, deck railings, and cedar columns. The intricate columns mimic interior ones; each

AN ARBOR PROVIDES THE PERFECT SPOT FOR CLIMBING ROSES, AND ANNUAL VINES.

STEPS NEAR THE SUNKEN PATIO MEANDER TO A MINI COURTYARD WHERE DONNA GROWS HERBS AND FLOWERS.

was made from two dozen pieces of wood and topped with a ball finial. Deck floors, made of a durable Brazilian hardwood called Pau Laupe, gleam like the interior hardwood floors, while the railings and posts match the white paint of the home's trim. "When building a deck or porch onto an existing structure, you want it to look like it has always been there," Ebbole says. "The details should catch your attention, but not the structure as a whole."

The backyard project meanders from the sunken patio off the deck. Thin rows of bricks march between slabs of bluestone and wrap around to the side yard, flaring to create a mini-courtyard herb garden. A shady side retreat leads to the front yard, where white picket fences delineate beds of sun-loving perennials. Everywhere you turn, fragrant flowers waft in the breeze, wrapping the exterior spaces in perfumed air. "You always have to turn or take steps to see into the next space. You can't take in the garden at one glance, which lends a wonderful sense of discovery to it," Donna says.

From sketches to finished project, the Brightman's backyard now plays gracious host to parties and daily alfresco dining, as well as comfortable moments of quiet solitude. Where old and new begins and ends is difficult to tell. "The deck has formal overtones to it, as do the patio and courtyard, but the abundance of flowers offers a nice balance," Donna says. "It's just a space you can't resist using and sharing."

THE MAIN DECK PROVIDES PLENTY OF ROOM FOR CASUAL DINING. THE GRILL IS LOCATED ON THE SMALL LEVEL JUST ABOVE THE DINING AREA—IT'S CLOSE ENOUGH SO THE CHEF IS STILL IN THE ACTION, WHILE ISOLATING GUESTS FROM ANNOYING SMOKE.

FLOWER BOXES FILLED TO THE BRIM BURST WITH ANNUAL BLOOMS.

When transplanted Dutchman Rene van Rems purchased his Southern California home, he probably didn't anticipate the splendidly rocky road he would take to a spectacular deck addition. "I bought the house for the property," he says. "I just flipped over the canyon—it was glorious." Embracing the natural scenery, Rene reconstructed his home's backyard space to blend with the canyon surroundings, reflecting the environment outside while establishing a serene, personal refuge.

The project began with a complete home revision. "I knew the house could be better integrated into the landscape," Rene says. "I started with a plan based on Arts and Crafts design principles, to blend the indoors and outdoors."

After removing an enclosed staircase and an old deck from the back, Rene established the Craftsman style

CEDAR SHINGLES, REDWOOD DECKING, AND RIVER STONE AROUND THE PILLAR BASES ESTABLISH AN ARTS-AND-CRAFTS SENSIBILITY FOR THE ENTIRE PROPERTY.

PLEXIGLASS IN THE DECK RAILINGS PRESERVES THE HOME'S PRIVILEGED VIEW OF CANYON VISTAS.

with cedar shingles over the home's stucco exterior. A new second-story deck extends across the width of the house and is enclosed by a plexiglass-panel railing, allowing an unimpeded view of the canyon's spectacular wildflowers.

A broad, open stairway descends to Rene's most striking, and heaviest, addition. Mortared in place, river rock serves as a remarkable facing on foundation walls, pillars, and columns. The tons of stone create a soothingly natural sensibility that seems to blend the home directly into the canyon. With their muted tones and prominent presence, the stones provide a natural texture throughout the backyard and around the entire home. "I saw those types of rocks on similar homes, so I went looking," Rene says. "When developers were excavating land, I'd ask if I could take the rocks they turned up. On Sunday mornings, I'd head to the site and load up my trunk. Fifteen thousand rocks later, I have a house of rock."

The rocks were power-washed and then arranged for construction. Featuring a natural, stacked appearance, the stones are attached to their location by a fast-setting, nonshrinking mortar. Keeping a scraper and running water nearby as he set the rock, Rene ensured that little of the mortar was visible in order to preserve a sense of

AN UNUSUAL OPEN-PIT FIREPLACE IN THE DECK FLOOR SUPPLIES PRACTICAL AND VISUAL WARMTH TO AN OUTDOOR LIVING SPACE.

MIMICKING THE COMFORTS OF AN INDOOR DINING ROOM, THE DECK PROVIDES INTIMATE FIRESIDE MEALS IN A GRAND, OPEN ENVIRONMENT.

WITH THE GARAGE TURNED INTO AN OFFICE, A ROCK-COVERED PLANTER PROVIDES AN APPEALING DECK ENTRANCE WHERE THERE WAS ONCE A DRIVEWAY.

stacking. A lacquerlike sealant applied as a spray provides a wet, clean-looking appearance that enhances the stone colors and textures.

After the original garage was turned into a home office, Rene continued the redwood deck around the office and into a private corner where an open-pit fireplace invites visitors to relish the cool California evenings. The wok-shape pit uses custom-made gas fire rings and provides a premium spot for evening meals and entertaining.

Framed by a combination of river rock and deck edges, a small pond serves as a serene entry point to a garden that meanders toward the canyon. Along with lantern-style lights designed by Rene, the pond provides a subdued Asian influence that remains consistent with the Arts-and-Crafts style.

"What intrigues people is that these decks are part of the landscape," Rene says. "They are outdoor rooms, designed so they don't intrude."

Using his professional skills as a designer in the floral industry, Rene selected a combination of plants that injects colorful elements while remaining true to the native landscape. The muted tones of redwood and stone coordinate with nearby gray eucalyptus trees. Plants native to dry climates provide balanced dashes of color beside the pond and in pots on the deck. "In Southern California, water comes and goes," notes Rene. "Even the plants near the pond don't need wet roots to thrive."

Having re-created an Arts-and-Crafts oasis in the California canyon, Rene considers the experience to be an ongoing journey, even with all of the heavy lifting. "There's something fun about the process," he says. "It's infinite."

THE ASIAN-INSPIRED POND, BORDERED BY HARDY, DRY-CLIMATE PLANTS THAT ENDURE CALIFORNIA'S FICKLE SUPPLY OF RAIN, OFFERS A PLACID, NATURAL ENVIRONMENT. ACCESSORIES SUCH AS DECK CHAIRS PROVIDE COMFORTABLE RELAXATION IN THE GARDEN.

Durable plants such as lavender and sage provide a colorful and textural counterpoint to the river stone on a retaining wall.

Pagoda-style lights blend an Asian sensibility into the deck design.

With heavy lifting and a dedication to style, California homeowner Rene van Rems merged his home with the nearby canyon landscape.

HANGING GARDENS

Robyn and Don Cannon's Seattle home had charm and a sweeping view, but its lot was inconvenient at best. Nestled high over Puget Sound, their home clings to a precipitous slope so steep that their house sits well below street level. An approach to the front door demanded a 50-step descent from the street, while an entrance from a back alleyway required climbing down a narrow wooden

WITH A TOUCH OF EUROPEAN DISTINCTION, A BRICK STAIRWAY LEADS TO A NARROW GARDEN PATH.

SURROUNDED BY MANICURED PATHWAYS AND STRUCTURED PLANT BEDS, THE LOWER DECK IS A RELAXING RETREAT FOR DINING WITH COMPANY.

OVERLOOKING A STEEP HILLSIDE, THE SECOND-LEVEL DECK PROVIDES AN UNOBSTRUCTED VIEW OF THE LUSH NEW GARDEN AND SEATTLE'S PUGET SOUND.

BOXWOOD HEDGES
TERRACED PLANTING BEDS
EASY-CARE PERENNIAL PLANTS
DECK AWNING

The back decks, formerly the only accessible spaces outdoors, now form a double-level centerpiece to a European-inspired delight. As with a chateau estate, manicured boxwood hedges line the pathways and frame the ground-floor deck. With a fountain providing ambiance, the bottom deck now feels spacious and relaxing, serving as a place for secluded dining or group entertainment. The second-floor platform, with an awning for protection, is more intimate and personal, offering the perfect spot for the Cannons to appreciate their renewed little villa by the sea.

STATUARY, SUCH AS THIS FOUNTAIN, PROVIDE CLASSICAL ORNAMENTATION AND SERVE AS CENTRAL DESIGN POINTS IN THE GARDEN.

A NARROW, CURVY COURTYARD WRAPS AROUND TWO SIDES OF THE HOUSE, CULMINATING IN THIS REAR PATIO WITH A BUBBLING FOUNTAIN.

BORDERED BY A PROFUSION OF PLANT LIFE, THE LOWER DECK OFFERS A SENSE OF SECLUDED OPENNESS IN A CROWDED URBAN ENVIRONMENT.

staircase. "You took your life in your hands when you came down those steps," Robyn says.

Even more vexing for the couple was the tangle of vegetation and the difficult incline that made their yard space inaccessible. To enjoy their valued scenery, the frustrated couple used a double-level deck as their only outdoor living space. "We couldn't enjoy the rest of the garden," Robyn says. "We didn't have access to it."

When a winter storm broke a sewer line beneath their land, the couple was presented with an irresistible opportunity. The Cannons recognized this necessary repair job as a chance to revise their entire hillside into a European-style retreat.

Now, in place of the original forbidding stairways, broad steps in front and back create gracious new entries that lead past terraced planting beds, a brick courtyard, and alluring pathways. A richly colored and invitingly structured garden surrounds the two decks, creating a private, enclosed sanctuary.

Where there once was a tangled, rambling hillside, tightly structured terraces rise around the house. Embracing a continental flavor, the gravel pathways and interlocking brick walls weave around classical statuary. With the climate and the difficult terrain, Robyn highlights foliage plants over blooms. With flowering shrubs such as roses, the garden possesses perpetual color without excessive maintenance.

INSIDE OUT

A KITCHEN, FIREPLACE, AND COMFORTABLE SEATING MAKE THIS DECK AN IRRESISTIBLE DESTINATION FOR YEAR-ROUND LIVING.

A GAS FIREPLACE HELPS SET A WELCOMING TONE AND CONTRIBUTES TO A WARM SPACE WHEN EVENING COMES.

While many people refer to patios and decks as outdoor rooms, the phrase is used loosely to indicate a place for occasional respite. Cathy Fitzgerald and Ed Sterbenc, however, decided to reconstruct their deck as a place for full-time, outdoor living. Taking advantage of the mild Northern California climate, their backyard space is an all-day gathering spot that permits cooking, entertaining, and simple relaxation by the fireplace well into the evening.

A previous deck had little to offer in terms of family comfort. The redwood floor was disintegrating and a

lattice screen enclosed the space, blocking all exterior views. It was "as if we were surrounded by walls," reflects Cathy. Ultimately, the family decided to rebuild.

Having removed the old wooden floor and lattice screens, the family installed a low-maintenance composite deck floor. Made from synthetic material and recycled wood, the deck resists warping and cracking, doesn't require staining, and is readily cleaned with a quick hosing. A new lattice screen with wide spacing provides definition without disturbing a view of the adjacent garden. On top of the screen, a new arbor serves as an open-air ceiling.

A thoughtful selection of amenities and details transformed the deck into a true outdoor living room. An outdoor kitchen offers a refrigerator, sink, and gas grill for complete food preparation. Durable, weather resistant, and easy-to-clean imported Italian tile graces the countertop with earthy, classic style.

Establishing the sense of a homelike gathering space, a fireplace serves as the deck's centerpiece. Designed to evoke the rustic appeal of clay, textured stucco encases the bluestone hearth, and weathered wood serves as the mantel. Although the majority of the deck mimics the gray tones of aged redwood, a contrasting cut of rose-

WARMED BY A PROPANE HEATER FROM ABOVE, A BUILT-IN CORNER BENCH OFFERS CUSHIONED COMFORT, STORAGE IN AN UNDERNEATH CABINET, AND A VIEW OF THE SURROUNDING YARD. A WIDELY SPACED LATTICE SCREEN OFFERS PRIVACY WHILE STILL ALLOWING A BREEZY OPENNESS.

THE NEW DECK WAS DESIGNED TO INTEGRATE WITH THE STYLE OF THIS 100-YEAR-OLD HOME.

color planks resembles an area rug in front of the fireplace. This octagonal design feature helps define the spot as a family meeting point and makes the space feel more like a room.

Unexpected features complete the deck's evolution into a full-service, year-round family room. Six speakers are positioned in the arbor, providing outdoor musical entertainment without excessive volume. Also suspended from above, propane heaters warm a built-in, cushioned bench, permitting outdoor relaxation after the evening turns cool. With such amenities, the family no longer has a mere deck, but an outdoor room for all seasons.

ITALIAN TILE ON THE COUNTERTOP IS NOT ONLY STYLISH BUT ALSO DURABLE ENOUGH FOR CONSTANT OUTDOOR EXPOSURE.

DECORATIONS, SUCH AS THIS HANGING CANDLE LAMP, HELP ESTABLISH AN OUTDOOR SPACE AS A COMFORTABLE AND VALUED DESTINATION POINT.

A COMPOSITE MATERIAL OF SYNTHETICS AND RECYCLED WOOD PROVIDES A DURABLE, ATTRACTIVE, AND EASY-TO-CLEAN DECK OPTION.

THE BUILT-IN BENCH SEATING IS CLEVERLY DESIGNED TO STORE CUSHIONS, KITCHENWARE, AND OUTDOOR TOYS. HINGED LIDS MAKE ONE-HAND ACCESS EASY.

ENLIGHTENED ELEMENTS

For Chris and Lynette Shelborne the simple serenity of nature is the best retreat from a fast-paced, technology-laden world. The couple wanted a place where they could not only relieve the pressures of modern life but find peaceful quality time with their family. "We wanted a tranquil gathering area for our family," Chris says, "a place away from the distractions of contemporary life, where we could escape and entertain."

Turning to their own backyard, the couple envisioned a fusion of the Pacific Northwest's natural beauty and the calm simplicity of traditional Japanese design. Embracing a spirit of openness, the owners began without a plan, allowing designer Shelly Johansson to consider their yard her blank canvas. For the Shelbornes, the result is a soothing masterpiece.

Three interlocking platforms that seem to float above the ground blend into the landscape. With a clean,

REINFORCING THE INFLUENCE OF JAPANESE DESIGN, A TEAHOUSE SITS SERENELY NEAR THE POND, INVITING BIRDS TO ENTER AND BUILD A NEST.

SPARE AND UNOBTRUSIVE, THE PLATFORMS BLEND INTO THE LANDSCAPE AND PROVIDE A VISUALLY PLEASING VIEW FROM THE MAIN HOUSE.

INTERLOCKING PLATFORMS
KOI POND
GRANITE WATERFALL

Spare, clean lines define the corner bench where water, stone, and wood converge.

Combining nature and structure, the deck is built around a granite rock.

Floating over a koi pond and surrounded by natural elements, this deck offers a calm place for conversation and dining.

unadorned presentation, the deck creates a contemplative, calm openness. Echoing the simple corners of the structure, a single corner bench provides seating for guests or for personal solitude.

While the platforms may be the most striking element, blending nature into the garden may have required the most effort. The deck incorporates existing land features into its structure, slipping around established trees and reaching around stone islands. A 4,500-gallon pond is filled with live koi fish, and 32 tons of granite comprise a rippling waterfall. Delicate, visually interesting foliage, such as bonsai and ornamental grasses, provide color and texture while framing the stone and wood pathways.

The only prominent elements of ornamentation include a granite Japanese statue and a teahouse structure that serves as a birdhouse. To add ambience when entertaining and to make the deck accessible in the evening, the space features discreetly hidden stereo speakers and time-controlled lights.

A living fence of bamboo provides the final element of privacy and solitude. For the Shelbornes, the new structure offers a welcome sanctuary where they entertain guests, join their children to watch the fish swim, or merely spend a few moments in undisturbed reflection.

"Our yard has become an oasis of peaceful contemplation," Chris says. "The sounds of the water rushing down into the pond and the wind blowing through the bamboo have helped to erase the stress of the day."

THE GRANITE WATERFALL AND DELICATE BONSAI TREE REFLECT THE ELEMENTS OF TRADITIONAL JAPANESE DESIGN, IN WHICH THE STRUCTURE IS BALANCED WITH NATURE.

KOI LANGUIDLY PASS UNDER THE DECK, PROVIDING QUIET, NATURAL SUBJECTS FOR OBSERVATION.

2 DECKS

Options for building decks are endless, but there are a few tried-and-true rules. The well-planned deck always matches the home it accompanies. For instance, a raised deck might not work with a single-level, ranch-style house, but a low platform will. Take your lifestyle into consideration. For the entertainer, perhaps a multilevel deck with plenty of space for mingling is the way to go. If you're simply looking for an escape, a freestanding deck tucked away from the house may be ideal. Don't forget to consider special features such as built-ins—a well-placed bench or planter adds personality as well as practicality. When it comes to material choices, price may be the only limit. Today's decks are still constructed from natural woods including cedar and redwood, but many are now built with more exotic materials such as ipe or jarrah. Even synthetic decking offers a style all its own.

What is now a welcoming backyard ideal for hosting a variety of family-time activities was once a tangle of blackberry brambles, tall grasses, and remnants of the forest that claimed the spot.

The homeowners cleared the brush while carefully preserving the native trees, including a stand of Douglas fir that soars dramatically up to 125 feet tall. Then, to realize the homeowners' visions of relaxing soaks, outdoor dining, intimate conversation, and children's yard games, landscape designer Tom Mitchell carved out a series of garden rooms. "We tried to make it fun to be in the yard. My clients wanted an outdoor space that was appealing and inviting," Mitchell says.

The first priority was to create a pleasing flow from the house to the yard, and space for comfortable outdoor activity. Replacing a small patio, the wide cedar deck hugs the back of the house and blends with the landscape. New glass doors to the kitchen open in accordion folds, creating a 9-foot-wide entry that provides easy access and blurs the distinction between indoors and out.

At 18×45 feet, the spacious deck allows for a variety of outdoor living scenarios and houses the built-in hot tub. Hefty wood arbors anchor each end, adding vertical structure and interest. Covered with vines that offer shade, the arbors serve as backdrops for alfresco dining and conversation. The dining area expands onto the deck's open center section for entertaining.

Raised 2 feet above ground level, the deck is a perfect height for observing the yard, gardens, and greenbelt

THE EXPANSIVE 18×45-FOOT DECK PROVIDES PLENTY OF SPACE FOR OUTDOOR DINING, RELAXING IN THE HOT TUB, AND ENTERTAINING. ITS LOW PROFILE AND THE SURROUNDING LANDSCAPING INTEGRATE IT WITH THE HOUSE AND YARD.

A BUILT-IN HOT TUB NESTLES INTO ONE CORNER OF THE DECK. A LOW, WIDE STEP MAKES IT EASY TO ENTER THE WATER, AND OFFERS MORE TUB-SIDE SEATING.

MULTIPLE GARDEN ROOMS

WOOD ARBORS TO DEFINE SEATING AREAS

BUILT-IN HOT TUB

beyond. A large expanse of lawn around the deck provides a play area for children's soccer games. The swath of green visually frames the flowers and plants.

Working closely with his clients, Mitchell let the garden plan evolve rather than putting everything on paper first. "We had lots of discussion about breaking up the yard into separate areas, similar to the concept of a house with different rooms for different uses," Mitchell says. Beyond the green space, Mitchell carved the landscape into more garden rooms around the deck in consideration of the varied needs of the family. "Each area has a different feel, but it flows together nicely," Mitchell says. Granite paths and greenery link the distinct areas of the yard.

THE EXPANSIVE DECK PROVIDES AMPLE SPACE FOR CONVERSATION GROUPINGS. WOOD ARBORS HELP DEFINE THE SEATING AREAS.

DAYLILIES, LAVENDER, LUPINES, AND HONEYSUCKLE PRESENT VIBRANT COLOR IN A SUNNY PERENNIAL GARDEN NEAR THE DECK.

COVERED WITH SHADE-PRODUCING VINES, THE WOODEN ARBORS ADD ARCHITECTURAL INTEREST.

GRANITE PATHS FORM AN EASY, NATURAL TRANSITION FROM THE DECK TO GARDEN ROOMS THROUGHOUT THE YARD.

Although varied in its design, the deck and yard are foremost a place to gather. They are a retreat from hectic schedules, providing peace, privacy, and an ideal place for the entire family to play.

A MAJESTIC STAND OF DOUGLAS FIR WAS PRESERVED WHEN THE HOMEOWNERS CLEARED BRUSH AND BRAMBLE OUT OF THEIR BACKYARD TO MAKE ROOM FOR THE DECK AND GARDEN ROOMS.

SHADED BY A REDBUD TREE AND A CEDAR ARBOR, THE WEST END OF THE DECK IS USED FOR DINING AND ENTERTAINING FROM MAY THROUGH OCTOBER.

ELEVATED THINKING

With the towering height of their house and the steep grade of their lot, Tom and Lee-Anne Krueger recognized the advantages of a large, elevated deck. An outdoor addition connected to their main floor would readily fit their lifestyle, but they also wanted to avoid a design that overwhelmed their home's exterior. Using a creative combination of decorative touches, the Kruegers discovered that a thoughtfully constructed deck elevates both their outdoor living space and their home's beauty.

To avoid a top-heavy appearance, the deck is supported by a minimal number of support beams, leaving the ground space visually uncluttered and free for other uses. The support posts and railings are wrapped in one-inch pine to produce a more substantial visual structure. Decorative details, such as arches and plinth blocks at the column bases, provide an architectural sensibility that blends with the main home. "We wanted something original," Tom says. "We definitely didn't want it to look like it came out of a box."

The deck features separate spaces for lounging and dining, allowing room for family parties, breakfast in the morning, and casual, everyday relaxation. Partnered with the elegant pergola, lattice intermixes with the vertical railing spindles, creating a gardenlike sense of privacy. Balancing difficult structural requirements with thoughtful style, the deck provides an elevated state of intimacy. "We didn't want anything too big," Lee-Anne says, "so it had to feel cozy."

FEATURING SHADE FROM THE PERGOLA AND PRIVACY FROM THE LATTICE RAILING, THE DECK PROVIDES AN OUTDOOR EXTENSION FOR EVERYDAY LIVING SPACE.

DECORATIVE DETAILS SUCH AS ARCHES AND A PERGOLA ENHANCE RATHER THAN OVERWHELM THE HOME'S BACKYARD APPEARANCE.

A PERGOLA SETS APART AN AREA FOR DINING AND ESTABLISHES A RELAXED SENSE OF OUTDOOR PRIVACY.

LATTICE BREAKS UP THE DOMINANCE OF THE VERTICAL RAILINGS AND EVOKES THE SECLUSION OF A PRIVATE GARDEN.

Pergola for shade and privacy

Thickly wrapped support beams

Decorative arches between beams and floor

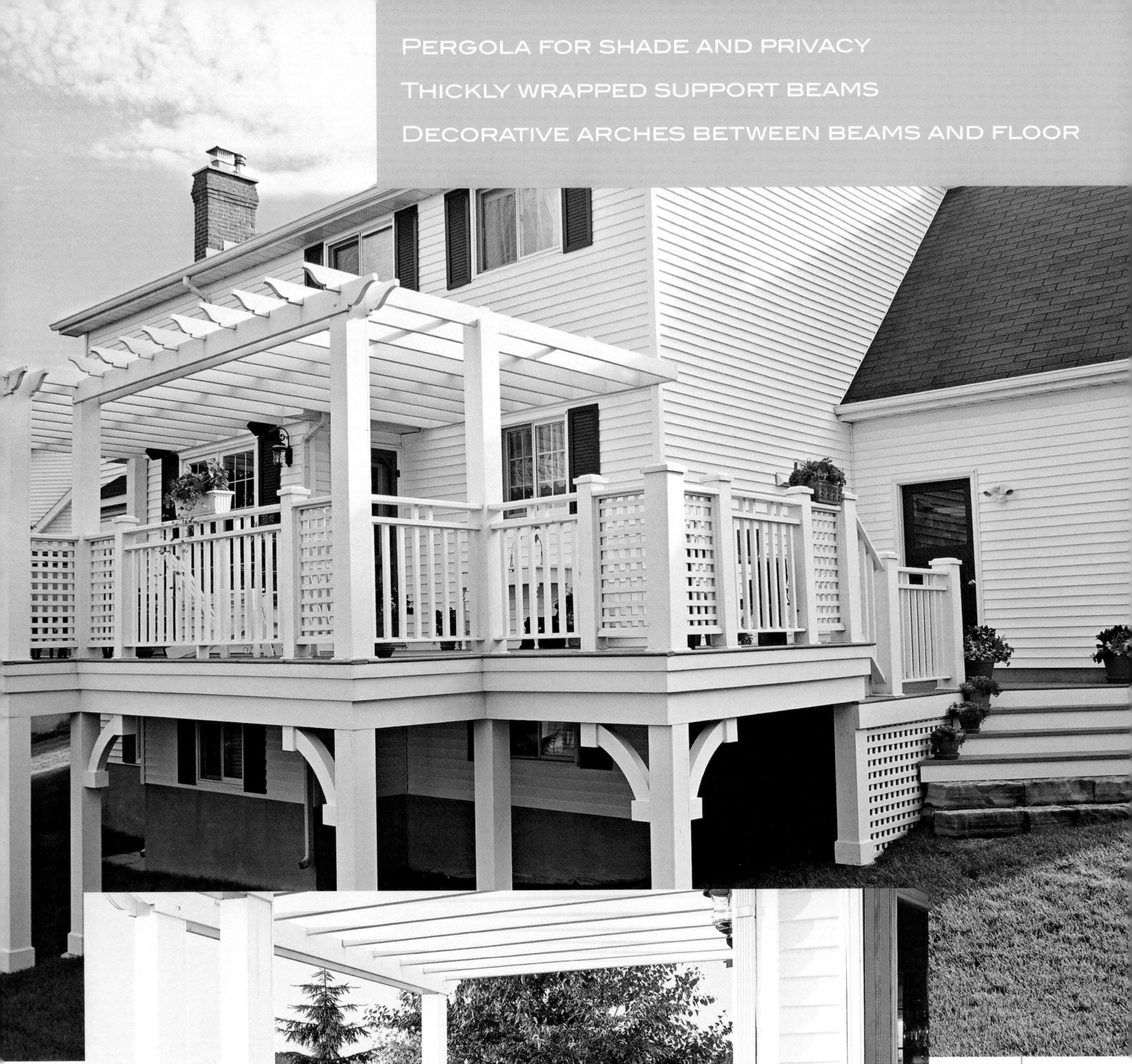

Where many homeowners are left frustrated with a yard where grass won't grow, Bill Dalton found inspiration. His yard may have been afflicted by poor soil and shade, but it offered more than enough space for a splendid backyard retreat.

Inspired by a train platform, Bill decided to construct an addition himself, relying on practical creativity to compensate for his lack of building experience. Staying low to the ground and following the slope of the yard, the deck features broad, welcoming expanses of wood that rise and fall with the landscape. The breadth of the deck evokes a boardwalk sensibility and invites visitors to stroll from beginning to end. Each distinct area on the deck has its own level. A modest rise or decline of two steps leads to a welcoming spot for sunbathing, dining, or tranquil relaxation.

Accessories and structural features define the character for each destination. Serving as space for sunbathing or entertaining, built-in benches create a notable boundary on the deck's edges. Since the deck features low levels and small variations in height, the Daltons rejected the typical deck railing. "We wanted to avoid the crib look," says Bill. Chaise longues, portable

THE DALTONS ENJOY THEIR NEW DECK FROM THE INTIMATE SHELTER OF THEIR ARBOR SWING.

SEPARATED ON A LOWER LEVEL, A SUNBATHING SPOT FEATURES COMFORTABLE CHAISE LONGUES, AN UMBRELLA, AND A SMALL TABLE.

LOW, BROAD PLATFORMS

ARBOR WITH HANGING SWING

BUILT-IN BENCHES AND PLANTERS

SEPARATE AREAS DEFINED BY LEVELS

chairs, and small tables provide the final, inviting details for each corner of the deck.

While the grass may be gone, the new deck offers plenty of space for colorful plant life. Pots of flowers decorate the wide steps and broad platforms, creating a mobile and personalized garden. A large, built-in planter serves as a divider between two levels, appearing as a discrete, low-lying plant bed from above and serving as a substantial structural fixture below.

At the end of the deck, an elegant arbor with a hanging swing provides the crowning element. Supported by a

SERVING AS THE VISUAL ANCHOR TO THE BACKYARD, A WIDE, MAJESTIC ARBOR ESTABLISHES A SENSE OF GARDENLIKE SECLUSION. A SUBSTANTIAL BUILT-IN PLANTER PROVIDES A COLORFUL ELEMENT AT THE FOOT OF THE ARBOR WHILE ALSO SERVING AS A PROMINENT DIVIDER ON THE LOWER LEVEL.

LOW, FLAT BUILT-IN BENCHES FUNCTION AS SEATING AND AS AN EDGE BARRIER FOR THE RAILING-FREE DECK.

wide lattice frame, the swing is the visual focal point for the new space, setting a welcoming tone and drawing visitors along the entire length of the deck. The shaded retreat within the arbor evokes the calming sense of a garden and defines the deck as a place for quiet reflection and conversation.

Rather than a bare, scruffy lawn, the Dalton yard is now a luxurious, personal boardwalk, as alluring as any green patch of grass and as comforting as any room in their home.

"DON'T FENCE ME IN" IS THE MOTTO OF THIS PLAT-FORM DECK WITHOUT THE TYPICAL RAIL SURROUND. "WE WANTED TO AVOID THE CRIB LOOK," HOMEOWNER BILL DALTON SAYS. LOCAL REGULATIONS DICTATE HOW HIGH A DECK WITHOUT RAILS CAN BE BUILT.

After Rick Younge and David Hopkins moved an entire Victorian home onto three city lots, they knew their garden wasn't going to be a simple hobby. Originally, Rick only wanted to "create a sense of order" out of the neglected urban space. By the end of their endeavor, however, they had transformed the lot into an elegant retreat of winding paths and charming shelters.

To one side of the lot, raised stone beds and a small pond reflect calming Asian influences. Edged by Japanese maples and pines, a stone path leads to a charming and unexpected potting shed. Inside this small shelter, a long countertop functions as a bar, creating an unusual entertainment destination. As the weather turns cool, the potting shed also offers an electric heating system that comforts both guests and temperate weather plants, such as a lemon tree.

The Asian theme continues farther back in the lot with a rustic, zigzagging footbridge. The simple walkway tames a perpetually marshy portion of the yard and provides a serene stage for ornamental grasses and Japanese irises.

Using another classic garden tradition, a side yard presents the orderly elegance of old English estates. A traditional boxwood garden forms a clean, structured space that highlights ornamental details and defines pathways. Beloved for their sculptural nature and hardiness, the plants are favorites of Rick's. "The boxwoods give us a wonderful green frame in the winter," he says.

Forming a tidy rectangle, the hedge formation guides the eye to another distinctive garden shelter. This tall, gabled structure, dubbed "the summerhouse," offers a welcoming, alcovelike retreat for quiet reflection among the boxwood pathways.

The final ingredient to this splendid garden oasis is a slender, two-level deck on the back of the house. From here, the homeowners can appreciate their garden's structured elegance and a vivid profusion of color while dining alone or relaxing with friends. With benches and a

HIGHLIGHTED BY AN ELEGANT GABLED SHELTER, BOXWOOD FORMS THE SCULPTURAL FRAME OF AN ENGLISH-INSPIRED GARDEN.

WITH COMFORTABLE SEATING AND A FOUNTAIN, THE DECK IS A SOOTHING TRANSITION FROM THE HOME TO THE GARDEN.

THE DECK'S RUSTIC FOUNTAIN SETS THE MOOD FOR GRACIOUS ENTERTAINMENT OR QUIET APPRECIATION OF A SPECTACULAR GARDEN.

Boxwood garden

Walking bridge

Gabled garden house

Potting shed as shelter

table, the lower level is a perfect spot to view their dramatic work, while the upper level supports a bubbling fountain that sets the ambience for a serene and comforting spot.

Having transformed a city block, Rick and David now enjoy the solitude and glory of a splendid courtyard retreat. Few on the busy street would suspect that such a spot exists in their crowded urban landscape. Whether finding quiet time on the deck or strolling with friends, Rick and David have nourished their own secret garden in the heart of the city.

SERVING TO CROSS A MARSHY PATCH OF YARD, A SIMPLE WOODEN WALKWAY ESTABLISHES THE SENSE OF A CLASSIC JAPANESE GARDEN.

A STONE PATH LEADS PAST RAISED BEDS AND A POND TO THE CHARMING POTTING SHED.

STRUCTURED BOXWOOD AND CYPRESS TREES ARE A STYLISH DIVERSION FROM NEARBY BUILDINGS.

SHELTERED FROM THE OUTSIDE CITY ENVIRONMENT, THE DECK OFFERS A RELAXING, SERENE RETREAT.

Elemental Endurance

The Pacific Northwest offers an ideal location in which to enjoy outdoor living. The temperate climate and rugged natural beauty seem to demand a deck of natural wood to blend with the surrounding environment. For Donna and Jim Wilson, such a deck proved to be not only the best aesthetic option, but also the most practical one.

Nestled in a timbered area of Portland, Oregon, the Wilson home is perched on a slope that dramatically descends into an undulating valley. Although it is a refuge for grazing deer and offers a glowing view of the meadow below, the backyard was virtually useless for two-footed residents. "Because of the hill we are on, the only thing to do was put a deck on," Jim says.

Because the new addition would be a major part of their daily lives, the couple recognized the need to build a structure that would outlast the elements and family life with two active children. "The deck really is our back-yard, because of the hill," Jim says, "so it was important that we did it right and then take care of it over the years."

Seeking to blend their deck with the surrounding forest of Douglas fir, the couple chose wood that would withstand weather, wear, and the strain of time. "We used only clear, no-knot cedar," Jim explains. "The clear cedar doesn't twist like pressure-treated wood, although it is softer. We're careful not to bang things around on the deck because of that."

Since the deck was a substitute for a backyard, it had to be large enough to accommodate the family's active, ever-changing lifestyle. Having already survived for 15 years, the deck seems to be a spectacular success. The enduring product is a gracious, 600-square-foot space that features areas for dining, family time, and solitude. Taking the steep hill into account, the deck is broken into two levels that allow for a sense of definition between a relaxation space and a dining area.

Despite its expansiveness, the design maintains

WITH TWO LEVELS AND A TOWERING WALL OF DOUGLAS FIR TREES, THE INVITING AND EXPANSIVE DECK PROVIDES SEVERAL AREAS FOR RELAXED LIVING SURROUNDED BY NATURE.

NEWER TREES, SUCH AS THIS SMALL DOGWOOD, PROVIDE A COLORFUL COUNTERPOINT TO THE ESTABLISHED PINE FOREST.

SET IN A FOREST OF PINE, TREES SUCH AS THIS VINE MAPLE ADD A PROGRESSION OF COLOR THROUGHOUT THE SEASONS.

81

a comfortable sense of privacy. A pergola partially covers
the upper level, making the space feel intimate and
protected. "We knew we wanted an arbor or some covering of the deck to give a feeling of enclosure, but we
didn't want to take away the natural feeling," Donna
says. "We can be out here at all hours of the day and not
get too much sun."

Featuring widely spaced spindles on top and lattice on
the bottom, the railing contributes to a private sensibility
without detracting from the view. Nature provides the
final level of enveloping warmth as new trees offer a
seasonal progression of color among the old pines.

Extra-sturdy beams in the pergola support several hanging plants and feeders, drawing several species of birds to the couple's personal backyard sanctuary.

While the structure itself fulfills their needs and has stood for more than 15 years, the Wilsons want to make sure it endures for years to come. In Oregon, maintaining the integrity of a wooden deck depends on the ability to resist the relentless presence of rain, moisture, and mold. The quality wood was a first step, but the couple frequently sweeps away debris so it doesn't have a chance to decompose. A regular coating of environmentally friendly, non-petroleum-based finish penetrates the wood and protects it from sun and water damage. The couple is careful about their product choice for both practical and environmental reasons, since any runoff

descends to their beloved hillside, their neighbors, and the river below.

For these homeowners, building a great deck was an investment in their lifestyle, and it is an investment they intend to maintain for a lifetime. "Many decks in the Pacific Northwest—with our damp climate and big trees—only last about 10 or 15 years," Jim says, "but ours looks as good as the year it was built."

A STEEP, UNDULATING HILL INSPIRED THE BROAD, MULTIPURPOSE DECK AND PROVIDES A RICH VIEW OF OREGON TIMBER IN THE VALLEY BEYOND.

BIRD FEEDERS AND PLANTERS MAKE THE DECK A SERENE PLACE TO REFLECT WITH NATURE.

TOWERING TRADITION

A CRAFTSMAN-STYLE LANTERN RESTS ATOP A ROUGH-HEWN POST ON THE RAILING TO GUIDE GUESTS' WAY WHEN DUSK ROLLS AROUND.

PROVIDING A STRIKING VIEW, IMITATION STONE COLUMNS SUPPORT THE PORCH AS IT EXTENDS OVER A MOUNTAIN SLOPE.

A LONG, EXTENDED DECK CONNECTS WITH THE PORCH AND PROVIDES A SPACIOUS PLACE TO ENJOY THE MOUNTAIN BREEZES.

The breezy, colorful mountains of North Carolina have always been a traditional escape from the summer heat. Mike and Linda Farrow loved the idea of a classic Appalachian cabin but wanted to maintain all the conveniences of a modern home. When they first entered these beautiful scenic woods, they had little idea that their project would take the rustic log cabin to great new heights.

With the assistance of architect Donald Wilson, the new summer refuge is an awe-inspiring fusion of the traditional and contemporary. "We always liked the look of a log house," Mike says, noting how the project reflects a rural Appalachian heritage. Roughly cut white cedar logs and knotted paneling create a rustic and natural appearance while the construction's clean lines firmly establish a sense of contemporary luxury.

As with old log cabin porches, the outdoor gathering spot the Farrows created offers room for friends and family to enjoy a summer evening. Their reinterpretation of a back porch features a balcony deck and screened-in room that extends over an adjacent slope, supported by soaring pillars. Jutting out of the trees and towering over the landscape, the porch provides a glorious view of the Great Smoky Mountains. "The porch sticks out like the front end of a ship," Mike says. "You get out there and there's nothing under you. It's a neat feeling."

WITH ROOM TO SEAT 10, THE PORCH OFFERS AN IRRE-SISTIBLE DINING SPACE FOR ENTERTAINING AND ENJOYING THE MOUNTAIN BREEZE.

CREATING AN ELEGANT TOPPING, A PLANTER WITH A COPPER RIM GRACES EACH COLUMN.

The spectacular structure reflects a desire to maximize outdoor living regardless of weather or insects. Connected to the kitchen and breakfast nook, the screened-in room allows the family to prepare a meal and easily slip onto the porch or deck to enjoy the scenery and mountain breezes. With seating for up to 10 people, the room is a favorite spot for dining and entertaining.

Wilson incorporated a striking stonelike element into the columns, posts, and railings. While this integrates a natural, earthy feature into the design, it also serves to provide visual weight. Wooden pillars could have supported the towering porch's weight but would not have matched the substantial style of the house. For Wilson, such a project with wooden pillars "looks like a bunch of decking sitting on toothpicks."

Although the work looks like natural stone, the columns are actually tubular steel piers encased in plywood and a facing of molded concrete. To achieve the stonelike effect, concrete is mixed with synthetic ingredients and pigment. The concrete is then cast in molds made from real stones. Creating the grand impression of a mountain lodge, the process establishes style and softens the budget. Since the concrete stones are lighter than real stones, installation costs are much lower, particularly with such challenging inclines and heights. "If no one had told you it was man-made," builder Harley Stewart says, "you would never have known."

Adding to the fusion of rustic and modern sensibilities, the stone facing and cedar wood is matched with copper details. The metal adds an earthy touch that ages gracefully. Along the deck railings, the stonelike posts feature elegant, copper-rim planters. Throughout the growing season, the planters feature flowering annuals, but when cool weather arrives, copper lids grace the posts.

Since their time at the house is seasonal, the Farrows rely on hardy, low-maintenance plants and try to preserve the native ones, particularly because they cherish the change of colors. Whether it is in the cool breezes of summer or among the tones of autumn, the Farrows have a grand view from their own side of the mountain.

THE HOME BOASTS ALL THE MODERN CONVENIENCES INSIDE, YET THE ENTRANCE'S WHITE CEDAR RAFTERS ESTABLISH A RUSTIC TONE.

ALTHOUGH THE FACING LOOKS LIKE REAL STONE, IT'S ACTUALLY CONSTRUCTED FROM A MANUFACTURED CONCRETE VENEER THAT WEIGHS SUBSTANTIALLY LESS THAN REAL STONE BUT OFFERS A NATURAL APPEARANCE.

IMBUING THE SUMMER HOME WITH TRADITIONAL MOUNTAIN CHARM, A STONE STAIRWAY LEADS TO AN ENTRYWAY SUPPORTED BY WHITE CEDAR PILLARS.

Northern Comfort

Although Ian Macpherson and Eric Gelling admired the 60-year-old rock garden that came with their British Columbia home, they could barely find a way to enjoy it. When exiting their back door, they were confronted by a rapidly rising hill that could hardly be climbed, much less used for entertainment or further gardening. "It was awkward and silly," Ian admits.

Rather than giving up on the yard's difficult qualities, they designed a new deck that uses the hill and its

STONES JUTTING FROM THE DECK ADD PERSONALITY AND FURTHER THE ROCK GARDEN THEME.

RATHER THAN HIDING AN ESTABLISHED ROCK GARDEN, THE TERRACED DECK FRAMES AND ENHANCES THE SPACE'S NATURE-INSPIRED SERENITY.

stones to its advantage, redefining the entire space. The three-tier wooden structure begins with a path from the house to the garden and then ascends the hill with terraced platforms. Rather than dismantling the established rock garden, the deck weaves around trees and boulders, using the stones as a focal point.

The once-inaccessible garden is now an inviting retreat for entertaining and relaxation. Deck platforms serve as destinations for conversation and dining while gravel pathways wind through the stone features. Lattice panels positioned as screens divide areas, providing privacy, quiet, and shelter. "Best of all," Ian says, "we use this area 12 months of the year—and this is Canada!"

PROVIDING SHELTER, PRIVACY, AND STYLE, A LATTICE SCREEN SEPARATES THE DINING AREA.

ADIRONDACK CHAIRS ON THE TOP LEVEL OFFER A SPOT FOR RELAXING AND SURVEYING THE LANDSCAPE BELOW.

One of the most endearing features of Louise and David Luthy's Seattle home was their garage's rooftop porch. Reflecting their home's Craftsman heritage, the porch was an inviting family space, offering a privileged view of their neighborhood and a river rock fireplace to warm the space as weather became chilly. "The structure had probably been here since 1913 when the house was built," Louise says.

When a brutal windstorm tore the old porch apart, the couple intended to resurrect a replica of the original. But modern building codes don't always coordinate with restoration ideals. Confronted with the city's contemporary building laws, the couple decided to combine the old with something new by constructing an open-air deck.

As a first step, the Luthys decided to tackle something that was a problem in the old porch. "With the previous structure, so much water seeped down into the garage that everything smelled of mildew," Louise says. "We never stored anything of value in the garage." With the

help of designer Josef C. Piha, a concrete floor provided an unexpected answer. Although the couple was originally uncertain about the appearance of concrete, Piha discovered a stained-and-stamped concrete deck floor that creates the appearance of aged stone brick. Water easily flows across this surface to a drain at the deck's low point, providing practical functionality along with classic style.

Knowing they couldn't return to their original porch's quaint charm, the couple did want to recapture some of the style and allure of their former space. To evoke the

EVEN THOUGH IT'S OPEN, THE URBAN ROOFTOP DECK OFFERS PLENTY OF PRIVACY FOR DINING AND ENTERTAINING.

OFFERING A PRIVILEGED VIEW OF THE NEIGHBORHOOD, THE NEW ROOFTOP DECK EVOKES THE SENSE OF A PRIVATE GARDEN TERRACE.

home's Craftsman style, a stately, custom-designed cedar pergola along with a substantial handrail runs the perimeter of the deck. With wide spars along the top, the pergola and railing combination creates a sense of enclosure. A privacy fence matching the handrails completes the feeling of solitude within an open area.

When Craftsman-inspired lamps illuminate their deck, the Luthys now relax on an intimate terrace that is part old and part new. Even though they have lost an original space, their new retreat offers some of the same amenities, including a sheltered view overlooking their little piece of Seattle. "You feel like you're in a treehouse," Louise says. "It's completely rural in an urban setting."

LOCATED ON TOP OF THE GARAGE, THE NEW DECK SOLVES DRAINAGE PROBLEMS AND REFLECTS THE STYLE OF THE HOME.

CLEAR CEDAR PROVIDES RICH TONES WHILE THE STATELY RAILING DESIGN CONTRIBUTES TO A CLASSIC SENSIBILITY.

ESTABLISHING THE HOME'S OLD STYLE ON THE NEW DECK, DIMMER-CONTROLLED, CRAFTSMAN-STYLE LAMPS ILLUMINATE EVENINGS ON THE ROOF.

PROVIDING A SENSE OF CLASSIC DISTINCTION, STAINED, CAST-IN-PLACE CONCRETE PROVIDES RESISTANCE TO WATER AND IS DESIGNED TO RESEMBLE OLD STONE BRICKS.

PIXEL PERFECT

Cape Cod homes often bring to mind rustic quaintness and stylistic simplicity. For Dennis and Pat Reagan, adding a deck to their house on the famous stretch of land required some new technology and a little old-fashioned patience.

Although the home already had a second-level balcony, the couple wanted to integrate the isolated element into a personally distinct backyard addition. "We weren't about to just throw something up there, a typical deck," Dennis says. "We wanted something different."

Combining his computer and a little imagination, Dennis used architectural drawing software to precisely plan, design, and test new ideas. Armed with their own plans, the intrepid homeowners redefined their backyard's function and appearance. Extending the original structure with stately pillars, the balcony shelters a new platform that doubles as an entryway. Stairs descend to a ground-level patio that offers plenty of sunshine for the famous Cape Cod summers.

While using richly classic materials like mahogany deck floors and red cedar railings, Dennis credits technology for making the project manageable. "You can go into the computer," he says, "print out the drawing, run downstairs to the shop, and make a railing."

CREATING A RICH, CLASSIC APPEARANCE, MAHOGANY AND RED CEDAR BOARDS FORM THE RAILINGS. AN APRON ALONG THE GROUND IS PAINTED WHITE TO MATCH THE HOUSE TRIM.

AFTER REPLACING AN OLD BALCONY WITH A WIDER VERSION, THE NEW DECK CREATES ELEGANT OUTDOOR LIVING ON MULTIPLE LEVELS.

WITH TEAK FURNITURE AND FORMAL RED CEDAR PILLARS, THE NEW DECK SERVES AS A POINT OF RELAXATION.

WITH THE NEW BALCONY OVERHEAD, THE MAIN DECK PROVIDES SHELTER DURING INCLEMENT WEATHER, WHILE THE GROUND LEVEL RESIDES IN FULL SUN.

Use of architectural drawing software

Extended balcony

Combined entryway and deck

When the Colorado winters finally cracked their concrete patio, Norm Jumisko and Judy Haase decided that a new deck would cover the problem. Although they had originally envisioned a simple rectangle, designer Steve Sparhawk convinced them that the deck could be much more than four corners of wood.

Approaching the deck as an element to enhance the entire house, Sparhawk created a structure that embraces the front of the house and one entire side. Rather than a traditional rectangle, the redwood addition turns the corner and expands into a round dining area. Because of its location, "our deck has the appearance of a traditional porch," Norm says.

Along with brick columns on either side of the steps, a curved green-and-white railing adds character and complements the house. To preserve the broad natural shade of a favorite pine tree, the deck is built around the trunk, integrating the tree as part of the design.

The couple is so enamored with the new deck and its coordination with the surrounding garden that they enlarged their living room windows to provide a full view of the outdoor space. As Norm says, the new deck "is much more than a pile of wood on stilts."

EMBRACING TWO SIDES OF THE HOUSE, THE BROAD REDWOOD DECK FUNCTIONS AS BOTH A FRONT PORCH AND A PRIVATE RETREAT IN THE GARDEN.

CIRCULAR CHAIR BASES REPEAT THE CURVE OF THE OUTDOOR DINING AREA.

GREEN-AND-WHITE PAINTED RAILINGS ACCENT THE NATURAL REDWOOD DECKING.

RISING ABOVE

High over La Jolla, California, David and Phoebe Sackett have an enviable view of the coastline. Unfortunately, their cramped, disintegrating deck surrounded by dramatically sloping hills didn't allow them to fully appreciate one of their home's prime assets.

With the help of landscape architect David Reed, the Sacketts traded a rotting rectangle of wood for a gracious stone courtyard. Using concrete for the base, Reed placed California Red Mountain flagstone on top to create classic Craftsman style. The stones feature a subtle sheen, possessing tones of gray and beige that shift in quality as the sun rises and sets. "Structurally it is like a deck," Reed says, "but the effect is that of a grand terrace."

The flagstone is partnered with rich, dark mahogany benches that also function as railings. Building the sense of Craftsman simplicity, the posts are crowned with pagoda-style, opalescent lights, providing a soothing evening glow.

To complete the addition, Reed placed a path of broader stones leading to the front door, inviting guests inside and drawing the homeowners back outside so they may enjoy their perch above the sea.

PROVIDING A SUBTLE ASIAN INFLUENCE, CUSTOM-MADE LAMPS CREATE A SOFT, ELEGANT GLOW FOR NIGHTTIME VIEWING.

FEATURING A CONCRETE FOUNDATION PAVED WITH FLAGSTONE, THIS DECK OFFERS A CLASSIC ARTS-AND-CRAFTS SETTING FOR A SPECTACULAR VIEW. MAHOGANY BENCHES PROVIDE EASY SEATING FOR ENTERTAINING AND SERVE AS RAILINGS AROUND TWO OF THE DECK'S EDGES.

FLAGSTONE FLOOR

MAHOGANY BENCHES AS RAILINGS

PAGODA-STYLE POST LAMPS

Originally, Howard Butzer and Bob Wimmer intended to tame the precipitous slope behind their house by creating a hillside garden. Although Howard is a dedicated gardener, they soon realized that the challenging lot was destined for another purpose. "It was impossible," Howard says. "The slope was just too steep and the ground is rock-hard clay, like cement."

After seeing a deck created by their neighbor Bill Nelson, they asked the former cabinetmaker to remake their backyard into a more accessible outdoor living space. Referencing the home's contemporary style, Nelson designed a multilevel deck that incorporates three separate platforms linked by stairs. The stairs snake around the hill's natural contours and provide distinct destination points for dining and relaxation. From a long bottom platform with a table and grill, the landing turns toward steps that ascend to an octagonal deck containing colorful varieties of potted flowers. Rising further to a perch enveloped by trees, the highest platform features an angled balcony for outdoor dining.

Displaying Nelson's woodworking expertise, the new structure is a convergence of practical construction and subtle craftsmanship. Posts and railings are beveled, edges are dressed with trim, and angled planks highlight landings. Built-in benches are crafted from leftover cedar wood scraps, providing a custom-made element that eliminates the need for moving furniture up and down the steps. Featuring a design of nested squares, the midlevel platform offers a bold, eye-catching stop during the ascent up the steps.

For complete everyday, all-day usage, the structure features charming enclosed lighting along the walkways.

A LUSH COLLECTION OF PLANTS BRINGS COLOR TO THE DECK DURING DAYLIGHT, WHILE ENCLOSED LIGHTING MAKES THE DECK ACCESSIBLE AT NIGHT.

A NESTING SQUARE DESIGN CREATES A BOLD PRESENTATION AS THE STEPS ASCEND TO THE SECOND LANDING.

MULTIPLE LEVELS SPAN A DIFFICULT HILL AND PROVIDE SPACE FOR POTTED GARDENING, ENTERTAINING, AND DINING.

Even more conveniently, the upper level includes running water and wiring for easy dining, quick plant watering, or simple cleaning. "Bill suggested we run wiring and plumbing up here from the start, so we'd really make full use of the space," Howard says. "It was a great idea."

Nelson's ideas have proven to be dramatically useful, with design creativity overcoming a forbiddingly difficult lot. The deck structure is so practical and attractive that it draws the homeowners outside day and night, whether for grilling on the lower level, gardening on the second, or entertaining at the top. "One of our favorite things is

having breakfast with friends on summer weekends," Howard says. "We plug in two Belgian waffle irons and make waffles right on the top deck."

WITH PLUMBING BUILT INTO THE STRUCTURE, PLANTS ARE EASILY WATERED, CARED FOR, AND ALLOWED TO FLOURISH IN THE SHELTERED AREA.

CONSTRUCTED FROM SCRAP CEDAR, A BUILT-IN BENCH PROVIDES A CONVENIENT, CUSTOM-MADE ELEMENT THAT EPITOMIZES THE WELL-CRAFTED CHARACTER OF THE DECK.

On a sunny deck behind her house, Susan Latter shares a glass of lemonade with friend and neighbor Carol Ager. They discuss the state of the weather, weeds in the garden, and flowers in bloom. After a while, Carol tromps down the stone-lined path leading to a gated arbor between the two yards. While the avid gardeners share a long, 240-foot property line in a rural corner of Washington, 20 miles northeast of Seattle, it is on Susan's expansive outdoor deck that they find themselves together most often, enjoying coffee or sunset drinks with their husbands.

When the couples settled in at their respective homes two decades ago, there was little in the way of gardens—or decks—to join them. "There was nothing but pasture here when we came 19 years ago," Susan says. "We moved in a week apart. We each have an acre and a quarter, so the first year we just mowed. When we began to garden, we would meet at garden club get-togethers, and we soon became friends."

As Susan and Carol's homes transitioned through the years, so, too, did their gardens and outdoor living spaces. Susan designed an expansive, 1,600-square-foot

SUSAN'S EXPANSIVE 1,600-SQUARE-FOOT DECK WRAPS AROUND THE BACK OF HER HOUSE, WITH SPOTS FOR DINING AND RELAXING UNDER A PERGOLA.

STEPS TO UPPER LEVEL

Z-SHAPE DECK WINDING AROUND BACK OF HOUSE

PERGOLA FOR SHADE

SEATING NOOKS

outdoor living area; it includes a long, winding deck that wraps around her house in a Z-like pattern. The space at the back of her house flows from one rectangular area to the next, and moves up and down across multiple levels. Paths lead from the deck to water features, borders, a vegetable garden, and a seating nook, with a garden chock full of intimate flower-filled garden rooms.

Outside a back door and flush with the surrounding gardens, a teak table and chairs, sheltered by an umbrella, welcome meals or relaxing moments. A quick turn one way leads to another table, shaded by an overhanging tree, that allows the two couples to gather for dinner amidst the summer breezes. Turn the corner the opposite way, take three steps up, and an overhead arbor shields relaxing chaise longues from sunny, hot days.

The steps add just enough visual variety to the uniform redwood surfaces, and provide the added practical benefit of allowing Susan, a native of England, more space to nourish her green thumb and her experiments with plants and traditional garden designs. Potted plants define the deck and outdoor living area. Containers line the steps and fill up corners outside the home's doorways, too. A plant stand with three shelves adds even more spots to display pots, as well as a collection of watering cans. The two women share time in

THE TABLE ON THE LOWER LEVEL OF THE LATTERS' DECK OFFERS A QUIET SPOT FOR ALFRESCO MEALS.

BUILDING THE DECK TO ACCOMMODATE THE YARD'S LARGE TREES AND MAINTAINING GROUPINGS OF CONTAINER PLANTS ENSURES A SMOOTH TRANSITION BETWEEN DECK AND GARDEN.

TWO CHAIRS NESTLE UNDER A SHADED SEATING AREA IN SUSAN'S YARD, ONE OF SEVERAL GARDEN ROOMS ON THE PROPERTY.

113

Stone stairs lead from the corner of the deck to the lush, intimate garden rooms beyond. Planted pots and petite stone sculptures add interest.

Carol's outdoor living space, a sunny deck behind her house, has a panoramic view of her hillside garden. A collection of potted plants helps define the deck and outdoor living area.

Many simple paths, which were originally beaten by susan's dogs, travel among the garden areas.

Susan's greenhouse and potting shed, which her husband, Barry, built for her on the back of the property.

The two gardeners hold in common friendly times and an all-organic attitude. "We're organic gardeners," Carol says. "We feed the soil, and the gardens pretty much maintain themselves. We compost and mulch, and that's about it for fertilizing and weed control."

Their gardening practices are distinctly different, however. Carol's designs tend toward distinctly open, parklike landscapes, with low-maintenance perennials, ornamental grasses, conifers, and flowering shrubs and trees. She has a sunny outdoor living space in which to enjoy her outdoor haven, with a back deck that provides a panoramic view of her hillside garden and hot red tuberous begonias that trail from an overhead pergola.

The decks are just one more element in a shared, easy friendship, fostered by a joint property line. Their side-by-side gardens allow Carol and Susan to exchange a love of growing things while they celebrate their differences. "We're just lucky to have somebody over the fence who thinks the same way. It's a great friendship," Susan says.

SEASIDE RETREAT

Creating a garden by the ocean presents its own set of challenges. There's the sun, sand, and weather, as well as the wear and tear from sea breezes and storms. With the construction of any hardscape elements, whether deck, patio, or other structure, it's not necessarily an owner or contractor in charge, so much as Mother Nature making the decisions.

Such was the case when horticulturalist Linda Pinkham and her husband, landscape designer Bill Pinkham, created a deck and pergola for this Virginia Beach, Virginia, home. The outdoor space needed to

capitalize on stunning views of the Atlantic Ocean and beach, both just a short walk from the backyard. But to create the seaside retreat, the couple was required to ensure public access along a path, while shielding the owners from the watchful eyes of curious beachgoers.

The Pinkhams, who have created coastal gardens for 27 years, familiarized themselves with this particular

THE CLASSIC, CIRCULAR SHAPE OF THE WEATHER-GRAYED DECK ALLOWS BURSTS OF COLORFUL BLOOMS TO SPILL OVER THE EDGES.

Simple deck to blend with landscape

Low plantings for privacy and ocean views

Pergola for shade

property's location and climate, including spots protected from the wind, the patterns of sun and shade, and areas that suffered most during storms.

Outside the back of the house, a rectangular pergola meanders along sliding doors. Its painted white finish matches the home's trim and complements the shake-shingle exterior. A circular deck, constructed of weathered-gray flooring, smoothly transitions to the seaside plantings, its curves echoed in the mounding billows of flowers, foliage, and containers. The deck's classic form allows the scenery to stand out, and the simple wood table and chairs provide the perfect spot for seaside views.

Perennials that bloom simultaneously for a summer color show, as well as withstand the effects of salt and wind, flow over the deck's edges, melding the lines of hardscape and landscape. The Pinkhams used a variety of plants to screen the public access path, creating

privacy with Hollywood juniper and Japanese black pine and adding a windscreen. "We try not to plant a whole row of just one type of plant because if the elements or disease strike, the whole windscreen may be wiped out and you have to start over again," Linda says.

In the end, the simplest of solutions—a round deck and rectangular pergola—work the best for the ocean setting, and plantings help to enhance, rather than block, the pretty-as-a-picture view.

THE OPEN PORTION OF THE DECK OFFERS A PLACE TO RECLINE IN THE SUN WHILE ENJOYING OCEAN BREEZES.

A WHITE-PAINTED PERGOLA HELPS TO VISUALLY CONNECT THE HOUSE AND SURROUNDING LANDSCAPE.

HARDY ICEPLANT AND WALLFLOWER, AS WELL AS ARTEMISIA, STAND UP TO THE SEASIDE ELEMENTS.

TEA ON THE TERRACE

Where many decks are designed as stylistic after-thoughts, this glorious Victorian terrace helps define the entire home. Rich architectural details and a visually dominating presence make this deck an integral part of the home's character.

Custom-built woodwork gives this structure a distinctly stylish personality. Drawing from the Victorian gabled roof, a charming open stairway leads to a broad,

inviting deck. Thick, substantial railings and balusters provide structural elegance while round, white columns firmly place the space in a grand architectural style.

Even more striking, at the bottom of the stairway the platform boards feature an eye-catching, custom-crafted herringbone design. Red cedar, Alaskan cedar, and redwood create a golden-hued, multi-toned color pattern.

The platform gracefully opens to the yard, displaying

honey-tone steps with a crisp, white backing. While the platform is unadorned, small potted flowers provide a delicate border around the edge and down the steps. A bottom step composed of inlaid stone completes the transition from Victorian terrace to lawn.

With clean, bright strokes and thoughtful details, this expansive deck defines the home from top to bottom, creating a refined terrace that welcomes breakfast with the sun or high tea in the shade.

EXPANSIVE AND OPEN, THE GOLDEN DECK PLATFORM FEATURES A HERRINGBONE DESIGN MADE OF THREE DIFFERENT WOOD MATERIALS.

CONNECTING THE HOME'S VICTORIAN ELEMENTS, A CHARMINGLY DETAILED STAIRCASE DESCENDS FROM THE GABLED SECOND FLOOR TO THE INVITING DECK.

A CUSTOM-CRAFTED BALUSTRADE ADDS ELEGANCE AND ARCHITECTURAL DETAIL TO THE STAIRS AND THE DECK PERIMETER.

Coastal Curves

Countering the boxy design of the home, the curved decks and mesh railing provide a clear, open view of the California coastline.

Succulents such as cacti add intriguing textures and shapes to the deck's sleek design.

Bronze railings are easily shaped and will gracefully age to a deep brown tone.

When designing a deck in a backyard with an inspiring view of the California coastline, architect Steve Adams understood the importance of creating a structure worthy of the location. "When you have a view of the ocean," he says, "you have a responsibility to take advantage of the free scenery."

After creating a modern saltbox-style house, Adams was determined to highlight the back. "I knew I wanted curving patios and decks from the start. I felt the soft curves would balance the boxy feel of the house and maintain the contemporary feel of the design."

With a foundation featuring stone facing and floor-

boards cut at a radius, constructing the curving deck platform was the easy part. The problem came with the refreshing sea breezes and the gritty, corrosive sea salt they carry. "I knew the basic wood deck structure wasn't a problem, but the curved railings were more challenging," Adams says. "I had to find materials that were weatherproof, would age gracefully, last for many years, and embellish the home's design. It also had to be pliable enough that it could be formed into curves to match the deck's floor."

After considering materials such as glass and cable, Adams settled on bronze, a metal that is pliable even when cool and may be easily ground to form smooth joints and edges. Using a hydraulic press, metal artisan Dan Burkowski shaped the mesh and prefabricated most of the fixtures in his shop. The pieces were then welded together and smoothed to create a long, uninterrupted line across the decks.

The result is a simple bronze mesh that forms a clean, bending railing with posts and caps. The linear metallic fixture maintains a contemporary feel without sacrificing style, efficiency, or convenience. Adding another earthy metallic element, a broad strip of copper flashing bends across the front of the upper deck.

While the railing maintains a minimalist sensibility, it also preserves unhindered exposure to the home's most precious feature. With wide spacing and thin rods, the railing permits a complete view of the ocean anywhere on the decks. The bronze fixture even seems to welcome the salty breezes. "It looks better with weather," Adams says, noting that the dark, burnished metal gains even more character as the sea meets the structure.

WITH THE TEMPERATE CLIMATE AND UNIMPEDED VIEW, THE DECKS OFFER AN IRRESISTIBLE SPOT FOR DAILY DINING AND RELAXATION.

WHILE ENJOYING THE SEA BREEZE, DINERS ARE SURROUNDED BY HARDY SUCCULENT PLANTS.

Easy Access

Designed for both utilitarian function and personal style, this wheelchair-accessible deck blends seamlessly into the garden.

The low, intersecting ramps provide shallow inclines, resting points, and space to integrate garden foliage into the design.

Creating a wheelchair-accessible backyard may demand code-required specifications but it doesn't mean sacrificing style. Rather than settle for a conventional ramp, Verne and Miriam Clemence created an accessible deck that helps redefine their garden space, making it visually attractive and easy for Verne to navigate in a wheelchair.

Embracing a spare, restrained sensibility, the new deck is flat, low to the ground, and highlighted by a confluence of gently sloped inclines. The visually intriguing coordination of ramps provides an easy progression

Low-profile, shallow ramps

Side bumpers

Short inclines

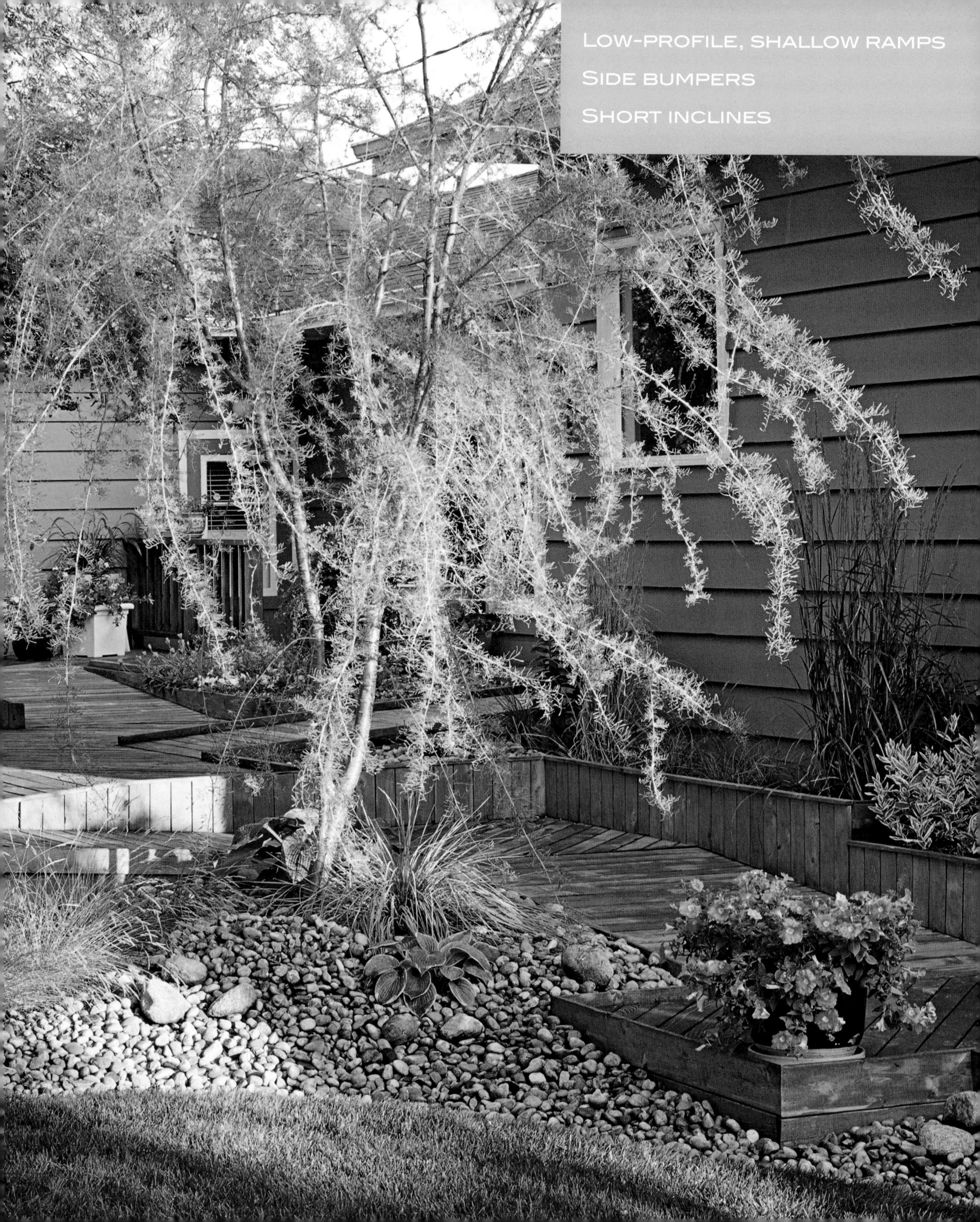

from level to level. Beginning at a broad sliding glass door in the living room, Verne may independently maneuver his electric wheelchair to a dining space on the deck and eventually to a flat garden path.

Stylistic decisions contribute to some of the deck's most notable and convenient features. The shallow pitch demands less effort and landings offer resting points after brief ascents. Small platform extensions provide spots for flowering plants while leaving the landing open and free from obstacles. Deck boards placed perpendicular to the slope and diagonally on the landings provide visual interest and extra traction.

A typical access ramp includes handrails, but the couple felt the railings would clutter the garden's visual presentation and believed they didn't need them. Instead, the ramps are lined with 2-inch-high bumpers that prevent wheels from crossing the edge and guide the wheelchair on landing turns. Since the ramps and landings are four feet wide rather than the more typical five feet, a wheelchair's footrests need the open space to turn without hitting a post or railing. "If we had a railing there, I couldn't make the turn because my footrest would hit it," Verne says.

The lowest ramp descends directly onto a path that merges the deck with the garden. A flat pathway allows Verne to move around the garden and enjoy the outdoor atmosphere without assistance. Creating a private courtyard, a high concrete wall features vertical, Asian-inspired openings that allow light and air to flow through the yard. At the street entrance, a cast-iron gate with a low latch makes it simple for Verne to enter, exit, and greet guests.

For the Clemences, their deck is the centerpiece of a personal retreat, offering style, comfort, and independence. While the rest of the world may not be as convenient, their garden is an inspiring merger of style and necessity from beginning to end.

WITH BUMPERS REPLACING HANDRAILS, THE DECK OFFERS A CLEAR VIEW OF THE GARDEN.

WHEELCHAIR-ACCESSIBLE RAMPS, DOORS, AND GATES ALLOW VERNE TO COME AND GO INDEPENDENTLY AND WELCOME GUESTS TO THE GARDEN.

SMALL DECK EXTENSIONS PROVIDE PLACEMENT POINTS FOR DECORATIVE FLOWERS WHILE LEAVING THE PLATFORM CLEAR OF OBSTACLES.

FEATURING AN ASIAN-INSPIRED DESIGN, THE CONCRETE WALL FORMS A PRIVATE COURTYARD WHILE STILL ALLOWING AIR TO FLOW THROUGH THE GARDEN.

Clearly Contemporary

An unusual home requires more than the usual deck. A simple rectangle of boards would have been overwhelmed beside this angular British Columbia residence. Instead, a distinctive home-and-deck fusion created from a contemporary collaboration of metal and wood fits the bill.

The platform construction echoes the home's angles by filling 1,000 square feet of space with long, linear tracks of wood. Like the deck of a ship, the wood follows the line

THE SEE-THROUGH QUALITY OF THE OPEN, GALVA-NIZED ALUMINUM MESH PANELS PRESERVES THE LUSH VIEWS BEYOND.

A BROAD STAIRWAY SERVES AS A GRAND ENTRANCE TO THE CONTEMPORARY HOME AND DECK. THE AREA UNDER THE DECK IS ENCLOSED WITH THE SAME WEST-ERN RED CEDAR SIDING THAT COVERS THE HOUSE.

131

of the home and provides space to stroll or enjoy different views of the scenery. Multiple levels and jutting corners define separate areas on the deck while a sweeping stairway stylishly connects the living area to the yard. Maintaining its contemporary sensibility, galvanized-metal railings with an aluminum mesh grid not only suggest modern styling but also preserve an uninterrupted view of the surrounding forest.

Even with its imposing presence, the deck deftly serves as a transition from home to the outdoors. Red cedar shingles from the house are repeated around the deck, making it appear as part of the home's overall architecture. Serving a purpose other than distinctive style, the angles and turns weave around an established 50-year-old tree, thoughtfully merging the old with the new.

The broad, expansive deck and its varied angles provide plenty of space for solitude or large gatherings.

The decking surrounds a 50-year-old tree, preserving a natural element in the secluded hot tub area.

3
PATIOS, POOLS & COURTYARDS

Outdoor spaces include much more than decks. Patios and courtyards provide durable, weatherproof surfaces for everyday outdoor living. Use your imagination—instead of a basic patch of pavement, perhaps you'll dream up a retreat of quiet nooks, open dining spaces, and extravagant entertainment areas. Turn a simple patio into an elegant courtyard with stone retaining walls. Or use plants to separate outdoor rooms—thoughtfully placed bushes, trees, and plantings seamlessly facilitate the transition from one outdoor space to another. Such indulgent backyard areas often include pools or spas—a patio's graceful curves are made to accommodate shapely pools in ways decks can't.

When the air is crisp and cool, free of mosquitoes and annoying humidity, Debra and Glyn Lewis and their family head outdoors. "Forget about summer evenings on the patio here in the South," Debra says. "The fall and the spring are the best times to enjoy the outdoors."

The family has good reason to revel in their outdoor space with the addition of a welcoming bluestone patio and massive fieldstone fireplace. The previous wooden deck that accompanied the custom-built house didn't fit the gracious European architecture. "The house called for something with much more weight and substance," explains landscape architect Will Goodman.

A glass door leads from the family room onto the expansive patio, with several seating areas that give it a distinct courtyard feel. A step down leads to spaced-apart pavers with grass growing in between. A low fieldstone wall encircles the patio, leading to the outdoor fireplace, which was constructed with a masonry kit that gives the look and longevity of a traditional brick fireplace without the care and clean-up hassles. A stone veneer blends the fireplace with the rest of the patio, while a gas starter, shallow cooking ledges, and a built-in firewood platform lend practical touches.

The couple now spends those cool afternoons relaxing by the fire, watching their five-year-old daughter play. It's a year-round haven for relaxing over after-dinner drinks with guests or quiet nights "to just watch the stars," Debra says.

A GAS STARTER ELIMINATES THE NEED FOR CRUMPLED NEWSPAPER, AND A STONE VENEER BLENDS THE FIREPLACE WITH ITS WOODED SURROUNDINGS.

A RETAINING WALL DEFINES THE EDGES OF THE BLUESTONE PATIO, WHICH COMPLEMENTS THE ELEGANT ARCHITECTURE OF THE HOME.

WALLED-IN RETREAT

Corner lots provide plenty of outdoor challenges, particularly when bordered by busy traffic on two sides. But interior designer Jim Walters turned the challenge to his advantage when he transformed his Spanish-style home's L-shape exterior into a series of inviting outdoor rooms. To accomplish the difficult task, he extended the golden-hued stucco wall of his 1,800-square-foot home

UPTURNED TERRA-COTTA TILES FEED THE POND WITH WATER FROM A SLUICEWAY.

A SPANISH-STYLE DOOR CUTS A PATH THROUGH THE GOLDEN-HUED GARDEN WALL.

outward, enclosing the gardens in a quiet, private retreat that evokes serenity.

The yard's perimeter wall stretches the length of the property, enclosing an outdoor area containing a variety of paved spaces, grassy areas, water features, and a pergola. There are dining spots and lounging areas, as well as nooks tucked away for further seclusion.

New French doors replace a street-facing window, creating a seamless transition to the exterior, and the living room opens onto a 10×10-foot patio. The view from the living room is not just a garden wall and rooftops, but a three-tier fountain that Jim and his partner, Bill Reichert, added. "Fountains are wonderful," Jim says. "They're pleasing to look at and are soothing. We have fountains in each of three different garden rooms."

Jim and Bill defined how they wanted and needed to use the space, and picked appropriate furniture. Each room has a focal point, accessorized with pillows and throws. Around the corner from the L-shape garden, a patio serves as a casual outdoor eating area, with

A SET OF FRENCH DOORS LEADS OUT TO THE PATIO, LINED WITH MEXICAN SALTILLO TILES. A WALL JUTS OUT INTO THE SPACE TO DEFINE A DOORWAY BETWEEN OUTDOOR ROOMS.

UNDER A PERGOLA, A RELAXING NOOK TUCKS AGAINST THE HOUSE, PROTECTED FROM THE ELEMENTS.

a round metal dining table and chairs. Jim opted against a patio roof; instead, an airy trellis supports giant Burmese honeysuckle that draws hummingbirds and releases a sweet fragrance throughout the house. A cast glass-fiber medallion finished in terra-cotta and flanked with sconces for candles hangs on the garden wall opposite the dining patio.

Jim designed a modular metal daybed that separates into an ottoman and two chairs for an outdoor sitting room along the exterior wall. Striped cushions in an all-weather fabric match the dining room chairs. A stucco wall, topped with roof tiles, extends the home's architecture into the garden, and paving stones surrounded by creeping plants give the look and feel of a lawn, without the need for maintenance.

A garden wall angles toward the garage and encloses an entertainment space adjacent to the family room. Its focal point is a lion-face wall fountain. The low partition intersects the garden wall at a right angle, stopping several feet short of the house to create a "doorway" between two outdoor spaces and to add a corner for yet another table and chairs. Again, Mexican saltillo tiles call for minimal maintenance.

Water flows into a small pond that skirts the perimeter in a sluiceway fashioned from overturned, overlapping terra-cotta roof tiles. Inside the pond, Jim added a glass dome for a spot of visual pizzazz. At night, fish swim up into it, adding a bit of nightlife.

Lush plantings and containers provide a transition between the hardscaping and garden. The tropical space is filled with birds-of-paradise, dwarf banana trees, palm trees, philodendron, flax, and hibiscus. "As soon as the hibiscus arrived, so did hummingbirds," Jim says.

In their honor, Jim and Bill renamed their home Casa Colibri: Hummingbird House. It's an appropriate moniker for the secluded retreat.

TEAK BENCHES SURROUND A THREE-TIER FOUNTAIN, WHILE TROPICAL PLANTINGS ADD TO THE LUSH FEEL OF THE OUTDOOR SPACE.

Outdoor Import

Much of Donna Talley's three-quarter-acre yard had been renovated—evergreens, arborvitae hedge, large perennial gardens—but there was one problem spot. An 18×24-foot unused space next to her Colonial-style house's sunroom sat unused, unloved, and neglected. Overwhelmed at the thought of another big garden to tend, Donna let the space remain blank, until one day she realized she had no good place to sit and enjoy the fruits of her labors. When her mother pulled a table into the blank spot, Donna had an "ah-ha!" moment, envisioning a European courtyard from England or France with outdoor furnishings and garden ornaments. "I wanted a feeling of antiquity," Donna says.

Donna used leftover full-size, aged bricks from a supplier because they were a less expensive option than new ones. Besides, "you'd never use concrete in a London courtyard," Donna says. The bricks sit in a basket-weave pattern on a 6-inch-deep bed of sand and gravel, with an 18-inch-wide earthen border against the house to hold plantings. A scalloped brick border on the two sides closest to the house lends a finished look.

Garden plaques and ornaments break up the large expanse of exterior wall, and a table, chairs, bench, and chaise longue add a wealth of spots to relax. It's a new space with a distinct personality—one that might be found in a peaceful London courtyard.

LEFTOVER, AGED BRICK AS INEXPENSIVE FLOORING

GARDEN ORNAMENTS

WINDOW BOXES FOR COLOR AND HEIGHT

A TABLE AND CHAIRS, AS WELL AS A CHIMINEA, MAKE
THE NEW PATIO FEEL BIGGER THAN THE ORIGINAL
EMPTY AREA. BLOOMS AND GREENERY ABOUND, TOO,
FROM POTTED PLANTS TO WINDOW BOXES.

WITH SPOTS TO SIT AMID FLOWERS IN CHARTREUSE,
PINK, AND WHITE, THE PATIO IS AN INTIMATE GATHER-
ING SPOT TO ENJOY THE VIEW. IN WINTER, THE WINDOW
BOXES ARE FILLED WITH BOUGHS OF HOLLY.

A FLEA MARKET FIND SCREENS A BASEMENT WINDOW.

147

Concrete Creation

Most families start and finish an interior remodel before moving on to an exterior plan, oftentimes not considering the relationship between the two spaces. But Karen Raley and Ted Galbraith knew that when they added a two-story space to their 1950s ranch-style house, a renovation of their backyard—originally just a concrete slab and swath of lawn—was in order too.

Instead of planning after the fact, the couple had the new part of the house built around the yard. It took 18 months of designing and professional help, but the remodel created an enchanting retreat for entertaining and living. "Walking up the stairs to the second floor of the addition is like being in a tree house," Karen says. "You're just surrounded by the garden. It's wonderful."

Besides new house plans, Karen and Ted met with landscape architect Dave Rolston armed with clear goals for exterior rooms: They wanted hardworking, beautiful spaces, great views from inside the house, and indoor areas that easily flowed outside.

The finished product is a backyard filled with spots to entertain and discover the outdoors, and includes native stone, a pond, a stream, and a fountain. The most dramatic change was inspired by a piece of slate from the home's interior floors. The old slab patio was removed and replaced with a large swath of concrete poured, stamped, and stained to look like the piece of slate. This concrete, which has a natural look and subtle texture, lends the appearance of flagstone to the yard. "People mistake the concrete for stones all the time," Karen says. "They always ask how we got such large stones into the backyard."

The old slab patio was originally separated from the garden by brick retaining walls. In the remodel, those walls were extended and capped with rough-cut gray stone, further echoing the hues of the slate floor. In front of the wall, a bench offers additional seating and a fountain adds the quiet sound of water. "The stone blends the concrete and brick and gives the wall an organic look," Karen says.

LUSH, INFORMAL BEDS MATCH THE FAMILY'S HANDS-OFF GARDENING STYLE. STAMPED-AND-STAINED CONCRETE FURTHERS THE ORGANIC FEEL OF THE SPACE.

Concrete pavers mimic flagstone

Retaining wall to define spaces

Secluded patio off master suite

Stone path through lawn

Containers dot the patio spaces, and comfortable seating ensures maximum use of the outdoor spaces.

Entertaining is easy with outdoor spaces that meld with the indoors.

Large pavers dot the zoysia grass lawn and a path around the yard links the master suite, patio, and an entertaining area, complete with a built-in refrigerator and six-burner grill. The view—whether from one of the isolated spaces or a communal seating area—looks out onto a recirculating stream lined with native Texas sandstone boulders and stones. Native or adapted plants match the loose, informal look of the yard, demanding little care but adding color, texture, and fragrance.

With the addition of 10 French doors, the family can host large crowds. "When we open our home, we can easily have 100 people here," Karen says. "Everything just flows." But the family also enjoys quiet time with family and friends in the revamped space. Classmates of Karen and Ted's nine-year-old son, O'Neal, are often drawn to the pond and stream for picnics and flower planting expeditions. They run from path to patio, from stream to fountain, enjoying the nooks and crannies of their delightful outdoor retreat.

"I had no idea 10 years ago when I moved in here that it could be so much fun," Karen says.

A RECIRCULATING STREAM AT THE END OF THE PAVER PATH DRAWS FROGS, BIRDS, AND CLASSMATES OF THE COUPLE'S NINE-YEAR-OLD SON.

COLORFUL FLOWERS—MOST OF THEM NATIVE OR ADAPTED TO THE TEXAS CLIMATE—FLOW OVER THE STONES OF THE RETAINING WALL.

The side yard of Helen and Dudley Fricke's home provided the perfect opportunity to turn a nondescript space into a well-used piece of the outdoors. Before the addition of a classic patio and fence, just a narrow strip, 10 feet wide, separated the couple's home from the neighbor's driveway. Today, that space is a whole different world, filled with a breakfast nook, pond, and fountain, spilling over with roses and sun-loving blooms. "It was wasted space, and now it serves as an outdoor room," Helen says.

Landscape architect James Furr's plans turned the miniscule stretch into a tiny, classically themed courtyard. A tall wooden fence could have blocked light and closed in the house, but Furr designed a unique solution. To enclose the space, a 7-foot-high fence lines the neighbor's driveway, while a brick wall faces the front yard. At the rear of the courtyard, latticework and a gate open to the back yard. Two sets of French doors—one in the breakfast nook, which replaced an original bay window, and the other in the dining room, which replaced a brick

wall—were added to the side of the house. They pull double duty, bringing in sunlight and adding a circular traffic flow between the house and the yard.

Large, light-color Spanish flagstone laid in an irregular pattern lightens the floor of the patio. Its mortared surface eliminates the need for weeding, so cleaning is a snap with a broom or hose.

Raised flower beds jut out in elegant rectangles or semicircles, not only adding seating, but also relieving the monotony of the long, narrow space. The rounded top of the front brick wall mimics the curved beds, while

THE OPEN BACK GATE SUGGESTS "AN INFINITE VIEW," DUDLEY SAYS. LATTICEWORK KEEPS THE VIEW LIGHT AND SUN-FILLED, WHILE PLANTS OVERFLOW BEDS AND CONTAINERS.

AFTER SEEING A SIMILAR DESIGN, HELEN ASKED FOR A POND AND FOUNTAIN TO SHARE WITH ALL OF HER GRANDCHILDREN.

artwork adds a focal point and breaks up the wall's expanse. Instead of an overhead arbor, sun-loving clematis and honeysuckle trail up trellises, and a neighbor's roses climb over the fence. Hanging baskets perch on the fence, hanging above light and airy, black metal furniture that adds a minimalist touch.

The couple use their courtyard from morning to night. In the morning, Helen and Dudley linger under the breakfast nook ceiling fan, enjoying the breezes, while indoors they enjoy the garden, too, from windows and doors. During the day, Helen and her grandchildren sit beside the small pond and fountain, watching fish and listening to the soothing water. The Frickes have even hosted bridal showers, club meetings, and family gatherings. "The courtyard serves as an extension of our home," Helen says. "You don't have to go outside to enjoy it."

BLOOMING VINES TRAIL LATTICEWORK BEHIND EACH SEMICIRCULAR RAISED BED. THE ROUNDED TOP OF THE BRICK WALL MIMICS THE SHAPE OF THE BEDS.

HELEN FILLED THE RAISED FLOWER BEDS WITH PLANTS SELECTED FOR FRAGRANCE, TEXTURE, AND COLOR. THE SURFACES PROVIDE EXTRA SEATING.

POOLSIDE PARADISE

When the owners of this "Spanish Modern" California home designed their dream house six years ago, they were adamant that they didn't want a pool. But after noticing pools and spas in other homes and in magazines, new surfacing materials, entries, and designs caught their eyes. They realized that a pool integrated into the architecture of their home and landscape could provide the ideal relaxation and entertainment area.

For help, the family turned to their home's architect, Norm Applebaum, who saw the perfect opportunity to connect the pool to the property by carrying the indoor architecture outdoors.

The space includes outbuildings—a cabana and an equipment house—that blend seamlessly with the existing home. The spa and pool areas tuck neatly into an ell of the house for shelter, with a fourth side softened by trees. The 44×20-foot space boasts sunny nooks and shady retreats, as well as plenty of practical details for maximizing enjoyment. "It's basically an extended outdoor room," Applebaum says.

Applebaum's attention to detail gives the structure a sense of permanence. The spa spills into the pool to merge the two, both of which are just steps away from the master bedroom and bath. A short, curved wall defines a sunny sitting area, and draws the eye back to the water.

Applebaum carried the home's Spanish terra-cotta tiles, white plaster walls, wide steps, beamed ceilings, and garden trellises into his design. The cabana's Douglas-fir roof beams extend into the pool area, while walls are made of smooth, steel-troweled Portland cement plaster. Subtle repetition abounds: Steps that lead to the pool continue into the water, and square shapes repeat in the spa, walls, and planter boxes that jut into the pool. Terra-cotta tiles overlap the pool edge, blending it into the hardscape, and smooth glass tiles

THE SERENE MIX OF WHITE, TERRA-COTTA, AND WOOD BLEND FOR A RELAXING RETREAT IN THIS CALIFORNIA BACKYARD. THE SPA SPILLS INTO THE POOL, AND PLANTERS JUT INTO THE SWIMMING SPACE. LEDGES AND STEPS IN THE SHALLOW END CANTILEVER INTO THE POOL FOR A SITTING AND SUNNING SPOT.

Pillow walls for soft edges

Spa spilling into pool

Pool surround for seating

Ceiling beams over patio

provide a backrest on two sides of the spa. The broad poolside surround serves as a patio for casual dining, conversation, and sunning, with plenty of teak tables, chairs, and chaise longues. An underwater bench, as well as steps in the pool's shallow end, cantilevers outward for sitting and soaking. "The ledge is especially useful for the young and the old—it's user-friendly," Applebaum says.

Today, the afterthought of a pool looks like it always belonged. The space is a welcome addition to the sunny California climate, with spots for easy entertaining and living year-round.

ROOF BEAMS JUT OVER THE SPA, AND TERRA-COTTA TILES EXTEND THE HOME'S ARCHITECTURE INTO THE POOL SETTING.

THE SPA, CABANA, AND PLANTER BOXES ALL HAVE SOFT PILLOW WALLS OF SMOOTH, STEEL-TROWELED PORTLAND CEMENT PLASTER.

It isn't often that paradise fits into a backyard, but in Patti Clement's case, a miniature version of a Costa Rican resort adds up to her own slice of tropical heaven.

Patti fell in love with Tabacón, an exotic realm of waterfalls, thermal pools, and views of an active volcano, and wanted to re-create the resort's magic in her Baton Rouge home. She turned to landscape architect Eduardo Jenkins, who had been to the same vacation oasis.

Jenkins faced some challenges: Patti wanted a swimming pool big enough for exercise, but her backyard was just 50×55 feet. In addition, a hefty setback from the rear property line limited hardscaping. Plus Jenkins needed to provide room for the home's buried electrical lines. His solution placed a long, narrow pool stretching 43 feet at an angle, integrating natural curves.

Jenkins exercised restraint in designing the landscape so Patti's backyard didn't look out of place in its Louisiana setting. Broad, flat stones edge the pool for seating, while a shake-roof cabana provides privacy for showering and changing. A shady porch overlooks a gentle waterfall that emanates from a raised, round spa nestled in greenery. The pool's Caribbean hue originates from a mottled, gray-green plaster treatment. A sand-color concrete patio topped with a textured veneer stays comfortable in the sun.

When Patti steps out the door to her backyard getaway, she is instantly reminded of Tabacón. "I come out and listen to the waterfall and light the candles [along the paths]. It's very relaxing," Patti says.

ANGLES AND CURVES STRETCH THE LENGTH OF THE POOL, ALLOWING ROOM TO EXERCISE. THE DECK'S TEXTURED VENEER KEEPS FEET FROM OVERHEATING.

THE CARIBBEAN HUE OF THE POOL COMES FROM A PLASTER TREATMENT.

NESTED IN GREENERY, THE SPA ADJACENT TO THE POOL IS PERFECT FOR SOOTHING AWAY ALL OF THE DAY'S WORRIES.

After buying a neglected 1905 brick townhouse, Gary Boyson and James Afflixico dedicated themselves to renovating the old St. Louis home. While possessing plenty of historic charm, the home didn't offer much opportunity for fully enjoying a summer day. "The floor plans did not relate to the outdoors," architect Stanley McKay says. "The backyards had service areas, but there were seldom gardens." To make the home more suitable for contemporary recreation, this backyard renovation balances period detail with a luxurious outdoor space.

Removing an aging porch and an awkward expanse of asphalt, the homeowners restructured their entire backyard, seeking an elegant and dramatic retreat. McKay realized the old yard needed structure. "The

house lacked an identifiable style," he says, "and also there was just no organizing principle to the property."

Drawing a line from the house through the backyard, McKay aligned the entire project from the steps of a sophisticated new porch, a defining feature. The porch

FEATURING COLUMN DETAILS AND STURDY RAILINGS, THE PORCH PROVIDES ARCHITECTURAL STRUCTURE AND A STATELY PRESENCE IN THE NEW PATIO SPACE.

THE PORCH'S DOUBLE DOORS OPEN ONTO THE SOOTHING HARMONY OF A POOL SURROUNDED BY BLUESTONE TILE.

165

provides a dominant architectural structure that easily transitions into the backyard and helps establish the home's style. "Screened porches can be a problem," McKay says, "because the screen is usually the major element within a smaller-scale surround. So we designed the porch to have a structural pattern defined by something other than the screens."

Stately trim columns provide a grand vertical presence, drawing the eyes upward to the balcony above. Large bronze lanterns add soft golden light to the patio while helping sustain the home's older heritage. Adding a cohesive decorative element, a starburst pattern forms a low railing and echoes a design feature on the front of the house.

A placid, inviting swimming pool forms the project's centerpiece. Aligned precisely with the porch's double doors, the pool provides the organizing structure McKay was seeking. Surrounded by a bluestone terrace and lined with a dark finish, the pool exudes a deep tone of indigo that is particularly inviting on hot Missouri days.

The linear design, beginning with the gracious porch and running through the pool, terminates in a curving boxwood hedge that mirrors the delicate curves of the pool. Cradled among the boxwoods, a fountain provides the final touch of soothing harmony.

Renovated and reborn, the backyard of this St. Louis home is no longer a neglected afterthought, but a summer-long retreat for all day relaxation. "We wanted it to be like a resort," Gary says. "It's like an escape."

HARDY PLANTS PROVIDE PLENTY OF FOLIAGE ALONG A FENCE THAT REFLECTS DETAILS OF THE NEW PORCH.

WITH THE POOL AND BOXWOOD HEDGE PRECISELY ALIGNED, THE REPEATED CURVING FEATURES BUILD AN ELEGANT SYMMETRY.

DELICATE WHITE FLOWERS AND SMALL STATUARY CREATE INTEREST ALONG THE TERRACE BORDER.

LEVEL BEST

When Gary and Mary Blum bought their Long Island home, the lot offered plenty of privacy and rich natural surroundings. But their yard's steep slope threatened to limit their chances of building an outdoor oasis. In order to fully use his space, Gary applied a little creativity to his yard, working with the hill instead of fighting it.

Rather than attempting to contain the grade with a vast retaining wall, the homeowners produced a level space using a swimming pool and decks. By building up one end of the pool, the yard becomes a two-level retreat with poolside lounging above and an athletic court below.

A tidy brick patio borders one side of the pool and connects two gray-color decks. Constructed of durable synthetic material, one deck provides relaxation beside a fountain while the other offers a bench and diving rock.

Natural elements such as stones and lush foliage form the remaining border, providing privacy, a screen for the athletic court, and a serene green ambience. "By bringing the woodland edge right up to the pool," Gary says, "it becomes an aesthetic feature in the yard rather than a rectangle with a concrete block around it."

PROVIDING A SUBDUED COMBINATION AT THE END OF THE PATIO, A SMALL DECK WITH A BENCH SUPPORTS A DIVING ROCK RATHER THAN A TYPICAL SPRINGBOARD.

CREATING A TWO-LEVEL YARD OUT OF A STEEP SLOPE, A POOL AND ITS SURROUNDING PATIO PROVIDE A FLAT-AND-FUNCTIONAL OUTDOOR RETREAT.

SURROUNDED BY NATURAL BEAUTY AND A SOOTHING FOUNTAIN, THE SUN DECK OFFERS AN INVITING SPOT FOR SUMMER RELAXATION. A SOOTHING WATERFALL WITH STONES AND GROUNDCOVER PLANTS FORMS A COLORFUL AND PLEASING POOL BORDER.

LAYERED EFFECT

Despite its grand 6-foot-high perimeter wall, this tiny San Francisco yard lacked privacy and style. Apartment buildings hovered over the property, and the bland stretch of grass offered little in the way of amenities.

For designer Penney Magrane, the challenge was to create a secluded garden with a functional pool within a restricted space. "Size was definitely a constraint," she says. "There was a delicate balance between having the pool the right scale for the garden, so it wouldn't consume it, yet still large enough for exercise."

Installing a pool that is shorter than a standard lap pool, Magrane positioned the fixture as a reflecting pool alongside a raised patio and garden space. Featuring delicate curves and tile trim, the pool extends to a wall where a Belgian lion's-head fountain evokes a sense of old-world sophistication. Sheltering the fountain and forming a frame for garden flowers, a pergola adds an extra dimension to the garden's identity.

Building from the pool, layers of plants coordinate with the structural elements. In combination, the carefully selected ingredients construct a private garden sanctuary out of a constricted backyard.

"Whatever a garden's size," Magrane notes, "layering is the one element you repeat that gives it both the drama of a mature space and a sense of intimacy."

ALTHOUGH IT IS FUNCTIONAL FOR EXERCISE, THE POOL IS POSITIONED LIKE A CLASSIC REFLECTING POND, LEADING TO A FLOWER-FRAMED FOUNTAIN.

ELEGANTLY LAYERED PLANTS AND STRUCTURAL ELEMENTS TRANSFORM THIS YARD INTO A EUROPEAN-INSPIRED COURTYARD.

ABBREVIATED POOL
LION'S-HEAD FOUNTAIN
SHELTERING PERGOLA

4 STRUCTURES

Outdoor structures contribute to a comfortable and stylish retreat. Gazebos, screens, and overheads, for example, provide shade, protect from the elements, and increase the architectural interest of your backyard spaces. Even an outdoor room requires boundaries to distinguish the space from its surroundings. Set up a table inside a gazebo to create an outdoor dining room. Arrange seating beside a trellis for added privacy, or use a pergola to provide overhead relief from the sun. For even more seclusion, consider building fences or walls to demarcate your personal space from the rest of the yard. Outdoor structures serve as prime spots for planting as well—allow lush foliage to peek between lattice panels, or watch as vines grow gracefully from the edges of a pergola.

Natural Cues

Juergen and Pauline Heise worked with nature, not against it, to create welcoming outdoor living spaces in their suburban Seattle yard, from intimate seating areas tucked into the shade of mature trees to a natural, flowing deck around their single-story ranch home. "I don't consider the garden an extension of our home; I consider it a part of our home," Pauline says.

The bones of the site were less than inviting when the couple moved in, but after much labor and love, the steep slopes and challenging soil turned into a blooming, gracious yard. The deck, particularly, reflects their philosophy of gardening in tandem with nature. Its shape forms a stretched-out Z, flowing from the back and side of the house, jutting out into the lawn, and gradually ending at a grapevine-drenched pergola that provides shade on warm summer days. Borders and island beds surround the space with a flowing, color-filled palette.

From the deck, a short walk leads to a small greenhouse and potting shed with glass panes and a brick floor. A rose-drenched arbor graces the garden entrance, giving just a hint of the inviting, relaxing spaces beyond, including a secluded cluster of twig furniture and an obelisk fashioned out of prune, grapevine, and wisteria-vine clippings.

In their new outdoor rooms, the Heises enjoy the company of friends, the music of birds, and the fresh breezes. "A lot of people don't realize the importance of surrounding yourself with beauty," Pauline says. "For me, my living space is my haven."

GRAPEVINES LUSH WITH BLOOMS AND GREENERY CLIMB AROUND THE PERGOLA, WHICH MARKS THE END OF THE DECK.

SET AT THE GARDEN'S ENTRANCE, A ROSE-DRENCHED ARBOR FILLS A SUNNY SPOT.

THE DECK FLOWS AROUND THE SIDE OF THE HOUSE TO THE SURROUNDING LAWN. CONTAINER PLANTINGS SOFTEN THE TRANSITION BETWEEN DECK AND GREENHOUSE.

Flowing deck

Pergola for shade

Potting shed and greenhouse

HIGH DENSITY

As his original deck of pressure-treated wood began to splinter, Dick Stewart knew he wanted something new and unusual for his Massachusetts home. "I wanted a deck made of something special," Dick says. "I wanted something that will last."

Little did he realize that his quest for an eye-catching deck would lead him to an unusual wood imported from the Brazilian rainforest. Ipe, pronounced "EE-pay," is a hardwood tree with wood known for its furniturelike quality. Because ipe is so hard that nails cannot be driven through it, each piece was predrilled before construction. "The wood is like a piece of steel," Dick says. "It's so dense it will sink."

But what ipe presents in inconvenience and cost, it makes up for in durability and a rich, fine-furniture appearance. With the demands of ipe, Dick carefully preplanned his new structure with carpenter Arthur Larson, walking out each angle and corner. They constructed a traditional cedar frame, then covered it with the ipe boards.

Stones are placed on either side of the entrance steps with the ipe boards expertly slipped between them to produce the illusion that the steps are floating or part of the rock formation. "We used chunks of blasted ledge along the steps," Dick says. "It looks like the wood is growing right into the stone. The rock went first, then Arthur fitted the wood next to it."

Although the deck offered a splendid retreat to enjoy the nearby timber, Dick felt it wasn't complete without a shelter to provide outdoor living in all weather. A year after the deck was completed, a gazebo was added. Providing a final unifying touch, the team constructed a table from leftover ipe wood and placed it in the gazebo.

With such a truly rare outdoor destination, Dick cares for the deck as if it's a cherished old cabinet, treating it with oil derived from rosewood nut.

"It's a deck," Dick says. "But the truth is, it's like a piece of furniture."

LOOKING OUT TOWARD A STAND OF TREES, THE NEW DECK PROVIDES A DURABLE, RICH SPACE TO ENJOY THE YARD IN ALL WEATHER.

Although it wasn't originally connected, the gazebo was constructed to appear as an established side room for the deck.

Combining the dark, rich wood with a stone element, the broad steps present a natural, inviting texture at the deck entrance. Supported by steel tubes hidden beneath the boards, the steps are fitted around the rock to appear to be growing from the stone.

Brazilian ipe wood is so dense that it must be predrilled before pieces are connected.

Although Don and Glenda Steele already had an expansive deck and vibrant garden, they felt their backyard wasn't complete without a shelter. To entertain friends and family, the couple wanted a spot that would allow them to enjoy their garden on any day in the growing season.

Ordering a ready-to-construct gazebo from a catalog seemed like an expedient and simple plan until the boxes

Surrounded by a lush garden, a mail-order gazebo transforms this deck into an all-day summer destination for the family.

Although part of the garden is in shade, groundcover plants, hostas, and statuary establish a pleasing, comforting atmosphere around the gazebo.

air during warm weather. A built-in stereo system provides music and adds an extra touch of luxury.

Now the gazebo is a preferred destination for birthdays, neighborhood get-togethers, and family dinners. "Our grandchildren's favorite thing is camping out in the gazebo," Glenda says. "They stay out there all night in their sleeping bags and they love it."

Although Glenda is already an avid gardener, the charming structure inspires her to even greater efforts. Using up to 25 containers, Glenda fills the deck area with an explosion of flowering plants that establish a warm, comforting ambience around the gazebo.

For the Steele family, a garden gazebo not only enhanced the appearance of their garden, it created a summer home in their own backyard. "We knew we wanted a gazebo big enough for entertaining, and this one has worked beautifully for us," Glenda reflects. "We live out here in the summertime."

GLENDA FILLS UP TO 25 POTS TO SURROUND THE DECK'S GAZEBO WITH GLORIOUS COLOR THROUGHOUT THE SEASON.

ORNAMENTAL GRASSES, HOSTAS, AND IVIES LEND THEIR INTERESTING COLORS AND TEXTURES TO THE GARDEN THROUGHOUT THE YEAR.

THREE STEPS AND NARROW GARDENS DIVIDE THE UPPER AND LOWER DECKS.

filled with lumber began arriving. Intimidated at first, the couple stored the pieces in their garage until a carpenter friend offered assistance. Within a week, the backyard room was complete and ready for guests.

Located at the end of their established deck, the gazebo is nestled among a profusion of flowering potted plants and receives shade from adjacent hawthorne trees. Serving as a dominant element in the lawn, the gazebo discreetly blocks the view of an extensive vegetable garden behind it. With broad screen windows, the room offers colorful garden scenery while sheltering the occupants from weather and insects.

Although the gazebo serves as a restful place of solitude, the Steeles also wanted a welcoming, tranquil spot to entertain and visit. The gazebo is large enough to accommodate a long dining table and plenty of chairs. When the weather permits, visitors may easily shift to the deck. Electric lights were installed to allow use of the space late into the evening, and a ceiling fan circulates

Deck in the Round

Sheltered by a canopy of trees, this cool retreat offers privacy from a nearby road, thanks to a curving trellis.

Thriving in the full sun, potted flowers provide color and block a view of the driveway.

The old deck had to go. After more than 30 years of use, Lynn and Howard Marshall's deck was shaky and dangerous. With their new outdoor space, the homeowners wanted to enjoy temperate California days without sacrificing solitude or dismantling the established natural surroundings. Innovative design and creative construction yielded just what the Marshalls ordered,

in the form of a massive, open-air room for all-day enjoyment. A need for privacy inspired the most unique aspect—a curved trellis seating area. The Marshall's property overlooks a neighbor's two-story home at street level. Acting as a wall, the trellis provides separation from the outside world without impeding daylight or airflow. A built-in bench follows the curve of the trellis and establishes the space as a destination for relaxation.

The circular seating and trellis were inspired by the existing stone wall that curves along a path below the deck. "I thought it would be nice to follow the same soft lines," Lynn says.

Rising with the landscape, the second section of the redwood addition serves as a gracious dining area. From this vantage point, diners may enjoy a view of the surrounding trees without the distraction of the nearby road. With a table that easily seats 10 people, it's the ideal place for entertaining. Subtle, built-in backlights on the stairs ensure guests can find their way between the two areas well into the evening.

Rather than standing alone as an isolated structure, the new design extends beyond the original deck's footprint to incorporate a canopy of trees for architectural interest and shade at the trellis level. The upper deck, meanwhile, receives full sun, making it a preferred spot for gardening. Flourishing in direct light, flowering potted plants add vivid colors and provide an attractive screen for the driveway below.

Spanning the length of the residence, the new deck redefines an entire side of the home. Stylish architectural details smoothly transform the deck into a grand

LARGE TREES OVERHEAD AND A BUILT-IN PRIVACY TRELLIS OFFER WELCOME SHADE TO THE DECK.

A COPPER GUTTER AND REDWOOD ARCH ADD ARCHITECTURAL ELEMENTS TO THE DECK ADDITION. THE GUTTERS GRACEFULLY CARRY WATER AWAY FROM THE HOUSE ROOF.

entrance. Copper rain gutters radiate out from the top of the trellis and are supported by elegant redwood arches. With exposure to the elements, the copper will age to a deep, eye-catching patina that will create a rich contrast with the redwood.

Mixing sun with shade, privacy with openness, and nature with structure, this deck finds an alluring balance. The shade of trees and the comfort of an innovative deck expand daily life into the open air. Regardless of the season or time of day, these Californians now enjoy their own endless summer in secluded splendor.

PRIVACY, SHADE, AND A CANOPY OF TREES CREATE A REFINED, INVITING SPACE FOR CASUAL ENTERTAINING.

A LARGE TABLE, IN ADDITION TO BUILT-IN BENCHES ALONG THE PERIMETER OF THE DECK, ENSURES AMPLE SEATING FOR A CROWD.

LANDSCAPE CORRECTION

For lack of a drainage problem, Bob and Lisa Merenda may have ended up with just another uninteresting concrete slab. But with a terrain that sloped toward their house, the couple was afraid of flooding a patio, so they hired architect Robert Gerst (now retired) to correct the landscape, as well as design an outdoor living area. What started as a modest idea grew based on Gerst's designs. "We imagined some little thing," Bob says. "Instead, he drew a beautiful big deck with a 14-foot gazebo."

The new space creates a parklike backyard that blends with the home's colonial architecture. Before building the deck, which bridges the gap between the house and the prefabricated gazebo, the land was graded and drainage installed. The decking, stained to look like redwood, is specially treated pine guaranteed not to rot for 50 years. For the floor, 2×4s were turned on edge, creating a tight butcher-block style at a height that's level with the house, ensuring a seamless transition from inside to out. The Merenda's new space ensures ample room for entertaining, lounging, reading—and even snoozing. "I fall asleep out there all the time," Bob says.

A SUNBURST INSET ONTO THE DECK'S RAILING BREAKS UP THE LONG EXPANSE AND ADDS CHARACTER.

THE GENEROUS 14-FOOT GAZEBO PROVIDES THE TERMINUS TO THE DECK THAT LEADS FROM THE HOUSE. THE FLOORING DESIGN, REMINISCENT OF BEADED BOARD, KEEPS WITH THE PERIOD LOOK. FLOWER BEDS TRANSITION FROM DECK TO LAWN, ADDING COLOR AND TEXTURE.

Breaking the Mold

It was a plain old, garden-variety concrete deck, just a slab provided by Pam and Matt Leeding's home builder. While the patio was fine for family gatherings, with a western exposure the outdoor space ensured that the couple, their friends and family, and the house sizzled on hot days. What the couple wanted, and needed, was a space that broke the neighborhood mold.

For help, Pam and Matt turned to friend and architect Jeff Hamilton, who designed a pergola of substance and style—one that matches the scale of the house and the sprawling backyard while providing a welcome outdoor retreat. "A small-scale pergola would have looked out of place," Matt says.

The pergola juts out from the house with large-scale posts and beams; part of its overhead structure is more

MATT SALVAGED GLASS BLOCK FROM A DAIRY, USING THEM TO PUNCTUATE THE TRELLIS.

A ROSE GARDEN PROVIDES A WELCOME VIEW FOR THE PATIO'S VISITORS. A BRICK BARBECUE AND A TRELLIS FACE EACH OTHER.

Custom brick barbecue

Glass block to filter sun and wind

Varied overhead openings on pergola

open than the rest, filtering the sunlight but providing shady spots for sitting and relaxing or sunny seats for soaking up the rays. Hamilton took care, too, to keep the view from the kitchen window unobstructed by the pergola's height. The open portion "lets more light into the kitchen windows below," Matt says. "When we want more shade, we put shade cloth over the covered area."

To the back end of the revamped space, the view looks toward a rose garden. A trellis along one side, punctuated by glass blocks, adds a privacy screen. Matt, a contractor, salvaged the blocks from an old dairy he was helping to demolish. He experimented with the pattern before tucking the blocks in here and there, leaving some openings to filter afternoon sun and wind without cutting down on light or fresh air. "I have a habit of doing things around the house that contain pieces of buildings we've demoed out. I always bring something from each job—stones, an old bike rack, whatever. Little strange things. They make the best story," Matt says.

The outdoor room's new focal point—a sizable brick barbecue that Matt designed—faces the trellis. The firebox contains grills on two different levels for cooking meat and veggies at the same time, and has a gas line for easy starting. Once the cooking is complete, with grill grates stored and a little wood thrown into the mix, the barbecue transforms into a fireplace for warmth on cool evenings or for activities such as toasting marshmallows.

After all the planning and work, the outdoor space turned into exactly what the Leedings had been searching for—a space comfortable enough for casual family meals but welcoming for larger groups as well. "We wanted the patio to be big enough for family gatherings and reunions," Pam says. "About 60 people come, and there is plenty of room to put out food, grill hamburgers, and let the kids play in the yard."

THE SCALE AND STRUCTURE OF THE HEAVY POSTS IN THE PERGOLA MATCH THE SIZE AND PRESENCE OF BOTH THE HOUSE AND YARD.

MATT PLAYED WITH PATTERN AND LIGHT BEFORE INSERTING THE GLASS BLOCK INTO THE TRELLIS.

Room Without Walls

As New England transplants, Claudia Schmutzler and Jeanie Werner endured their fair share of frosty breezes and frigid temperatures. So when the duo relocated to Southern California, they were determined to take advantage of year-round living, with its accompanying balmy breezes and sun-soaking temperatures. To do that, they needed to transform the ugly, dilapidated backyard of their 1960s home into a space that exuded personality.

Before the pair, partners in a landscape design business, dove into the project, they traipsed across the yard, armed with a tape measure and list of amenities: dining area, grill, built-in seating, and potted plants.

Gone was the original patio, with rotting posts and a wavy green plastic roof that flapped in the wind. In its place, a builder constructed a 12×40-foot outdoor room topped by a pergola.

Cedar wood won over tile and concrete for flooring, giving the deck a more inviting feel. "I wanted cozy, so I

THE DECK IS COLOR-STAINED WITH HEAVY-DUTY MARINE PRIMER, WHICH COMBATS DRYING AND WEATHERING FROM THE SALT AIR.

THE OUTDOOR GARDEN HAVEN SHIELDS GUESTS FROM THE SUN WITH A PERGOLA; A GRAPEVINE, AN IDEA BORROWED FROM A TRATTORIA IN ITALY, GROWS OVER THE STRUCTURE.

HANGING WALL OF WINDOWS OFFERS PRIVACY

GRAPEVINE TRAILING ACROSS PERGOLA

SEPARATE AREAS FOR DINING AND GRILLING

talked to my builder about it. He had considered using wood for his own patio but didn't, and he was sorry he'd gone with concrete," Claudia says.

The pergola, made of strong but less-expensive Douglas fir, shields visitors from days filled with relentless, hot sunshine. The covering extends to all but 12 feet on the deck's far end; that open space soaks up the sun.

Before the outdoor transformation, privacy was nearly nonexistent, with just a 5-foot cinderblock wall and several wood fences. Select elements—including lattice panels on top of the fence that borders the yard, a new tree in the back corner, and lush roses, bougainvillea, and perennial morning glory—now add a welcome screen to unwanted views. A trio of windows, left over from an interior remodeling, dangles from galvanized chain, blocking a view of a neighbor's home just 5 feet away. A valance, courtesy of a seamstress friend, finishes off

the floating wall. "All you see now is green flowering vines. You really can't see another house," Claudia says.

In addition to the profuse plantings, color abounds on the deck, too, with stain inspired by a wreath from a friend. The Eucalyptus green, cream, and brown provides a dense backdrop to the shrubbery and grass.

Five exterior power outlets, hidden by furniture or flowerpots, and small lamps attached to walls and furniture maximize the flexibility of the space. Seating near the grill allows guests to keep Jeanie company while she barbecues, and armchairs, a table and chairs, and a chaise longue offer space for dining and relaxing.

"I really wanted the deck to be functional, comfortable, and spacious," Claudia says. It's the best of all rooms—this one without walls.

AN ECLECTIC MIX OF POTTED PLANTS INFUSES THE SPACE WITH COLOR; THEY CLIMB OVER ARBORS, THROUGH CHAIRS, AND ABOVE RAILINGS.

COMFORTABLE WICKER SEATING ABOUNDS ON THE GENEROUS-SIZE DECK, WHILE SIDE TABLES PROVIDE AMPLE SPACE FOR BEVERAGES AND FOOD.

A RAILING HAS BUILT-IN BENCHES AROUND ONE CORNER OF THE DECK, WHILE A WALL OF FLOATING WINDOWS SHIELDS THE VIEW FROM THE NEIGHBORS.

The San Francisco backyard of San Tran and Dennis Durzinsky was a dismal space. The only view—toward a wall of stacked concrete blocks stabilizing the hillside to the rear—was broken only by the unappealing colors of a random assortment of perennials and container plants. And that wasn't all: The existing deck,

FRENCH DOORS OPEN ONTO THE WOOD DECK, WHERE A ROOF SHIELDS VISITORS FROM THE ELEMENTS.

SANDSTONE STAIRS LEAD TO AN UPPER LOUNGE AREA SHIELDED FROM VIEW BY GIANT BIRDS-OF-PARADISE.

constructed of plank and brick, was partially shielded by a roof. But landscape architect Richard McPherson saw potential in the space, which sloped upward into a hill and made it possible to create two outdoor levels. The new, transformed garden room is a treat for the senses, filled with a variety of textures and colors that add an aura of expansiveness to the urban yard.

Original access to the yard was via a circular staircase up from the garage; a neighbor allowed a portion of a privacy fence to be removed in order to provide another entrance. Newly poured concrete retaining walls, stained to blend into the surroundings and minimize bulk, were added to stabilize the hill.

McPherson kept the deck's original plank flooring, but extended the area outward with black slate tiles. French doors lead from the home's interior dining room out to the patio; if weather permits, San and Dennis can throw open the doors and still enjoy the garden greenery. A short flight of rough Connecticut bluestone steps leads to an upper-level lounge, shielded by giant birds-of-paradise and complete with a comfy chaise longue for relaxing. Walls, separating the upper lounge from the deck below, are sheathed in stained cedar shingles and capped with black-painted redwood.

A BUILT-IN GRILL CUTS DOWN ON CLUTTER. RAISED BEDS ABUT THE SPACE, WHICH SITS OPPOSITE THE DINING ROOM'S FRENCH DOORS.

AN OVERHANGING ROOF WITH SKYLIGHTS PROVIDES A PLACE FOR OUTDOOR DINING EVEN WHEN IT RAINS.

In a space so small, each design piece carries added importance; for Dennis and San's space, plant and hardscape choices were crucial. A built-in gas grill along the back wall cuts down on clutter. Wooden privacy fences and walls alongside the deck shield the view, while copper lights illuminate the steps to the upper lounge.

Subtropical foliage, ideal for the yard's hot microclimate, adds structure and color without overwhelming the small space. The raised beds on the stepped-up cedar framing, filled with contrasting textures of purple-blooming lobelia and spiky vinca, contribute to the secluded feel. Texture and contrast were more important in plant selection than color; lantana, bacopa, azalea, and star jasmine provide white accents; blues and purples come from campanula and lobelia.

A fountain, constructed of varying sizes of concrete cubes stacked at angles to one another, adds the soothing gurgle of water. Discreetly placed lamps highlight pygmy date palms and star jasmine. Low-maintenance, high-style steel furnishings, reminiscent of a casual bistro at a tropical resort, are the perfect finishing touch.

On the upper terrace, San and Dennis read the paper, while under the overhanging roof punctuated with skylights, the pair dines outside. No matter where they are, the heady blooms of flowers and textures of vines surround them. "One of the joys is sitting at the dinner table and looking out through the doors at night because the garden is lit," San says.

In the end, San and Dennis turned their tiny yard into a space for relaxing, dining, grilling, or entertaining. "We look forward to enjoying every evening in an area that has truly become our mini oasis," San says.

CONCRETE CUBES, STACKED AT ANGLES TO ONE ANOTHER, PROVIDE A FOUNTAIN THAT GURGLES WITH WATER. LUSH FOLIAGE IN VARYING SHADES OF GREEN SURROUNDS THE SPACE.

STAR JASMINE VINE ADDS HEADY PERFUME AND CLUSTERS OF SMALL WHITE FLOWERS.

CONTEMPORARY CHAIRS AND TABLES MATCH THE CLEAN LINES OF THE SPACE.

FROM SAND TO SANCTUARY

When first-time homeowners and first-time gardeners Linda and Iver Engebretson moved into their California home, they found a weed-strewn, unusable alley in place of a backyard. The swath—18 feet wide and 96 feet long—stretched around both sides of the home and was exposed to the second-story windows of four neighbors. The couple wanted a welcoming backyard, but had no idea what to do with the space they had. "We knew that we wanted to barbecue, we wanted to have a place for a dining table, and we wanted to have a spa," Linda says. "But we couldn't envision how it could be put together."

Enter landscape architects Steve and Katherine Evans. The duo trucked in compost and, in an innovative design, split the space into dining and living rooms, a breakfast nook, and a spa, which transformed the skinny corridor into a lush, secluded retreat. "This is a garden about space, not just about rooms," Steve Evans says. "We designed usable, functional spaces linked by transitional spaces and created the feeling of containment in the spaces. It's very intimate, and it works."

Arbors, pergolas, and paving define each room with height and pattern. A 5-foot-wide, arbor-framed walkway runs the length of the yard, its columns made from sizable 6-foot-10-inch-high stuccoed columns. A slightly different style of taller wood supports hold up the pergola in the breakfast nook, which also has a floor of concrete paving stones. The subtle colors in the pavers, laid in classical tile patterns, create a ruglike appearance, in contrast with the soft curve of the decomposed granite

A 5-FOOT-WIDE ARBOR WITH A FLOOR OF DECOMPOSED GRANITE LEADS FROM ONE END OF THE YARD TO THE OTHER.

THE SAND IN THE BACKYARD CAME STRAIGHT FROM SAN FRANCISCO BAY.

SECLUSION IN THE SPA IS MAXIMIZED WITH AN OVERHEAD PERGOLA AND WIRE-MESH SCREENING.

paths. Another pergola, interesting plantings, and eye-deceiving, welded wire-mesh screens shield the intimate spa area, which is set on a raised redwood deck. Blooming shrubs and large container plants add splashes of color and texture.

Two years after they moved, the couple turned their "negative space" into a truly positive haven. Iver now spends his Saturdays cooking on the breakfast nook's adjacent barbecue, and both use weekend mornings to catch up on deadheading their flowers.

"When we moved in, we didn't have any experience and we didn't have any expectations," Linda says. The yard "was just another thing we had to do when we moved into a house. Now, we're back there all the time. It's the most important part of our home."

COMFORTABLE CHAIRS ALLOW FOR PLENTY OF SEATING IN THE LIVING ROOM. LUSH PLANTINGS AND A SCREEN SHIELD THE VIEW FROM NEIGHBORS.

CONCRETE PAVERS AND A SLIGHTLY HIGHER PERGOLA DEFINE THE COZY BREAKFAST NOOK. A BARBECUE SITS ADJACENT TO THE BREAKFAST NOOK.

THE NOT-SO-BIG YARD

When David and Jane Rivera made the life-changing decision to tear down their 1950s ranch home, the yard that was left came down with it. The new home, set on the couple's one-eighth-acre lot, is not so big, and that space-conscious design extends outdoors too. The home functions larger than its square footage, in part due to the extension of living areas outside, which then offer the right amount of space to entertain and relax.

The yard's focal point is a channel that runs from one end to the other. A dry-stack stone fountain spills water onto polished river rocks. The narrow space, dug several inches lower than ground level, runs the length of the lawn, disappearing under the dining space's raised concrete slab before reappearing in a cutout underneath the dining table. It then disappears again, reappearing on the other side of the dining patio and ending at the perimeter fence. The background sound of water is soothing for visitors. Along the privacy fence, raised beds add color and height.

A minimalist back entry is covered by a similar-size pergola supported by four stucco columns. The simple concrete slab from that door leads to pavers in front of a

Outside a back entry, a pergola shields visitors, while French doors open onto a simple concrete slab. Fabric drapes surround a dining area.

The channel disappears under the dining slab, reappears under the table, and flows underground again until it reaches the far side of the space.

CHANNEL THAT TRAVERSES YARD

COVERED DINING PATIO SHIELDED BY FABRIC DRAPES

MINIMALIST MATERIALS CHOICES

211

series of French doors, which open onto a small expanse of lawn. Pavers continue to the outdoor dining area, connected to the interior living area by another series of French doors. It, too, is covered by a pergola, with eight columns—four to each side—that support the overhead structure. An overhead heater, similar to those used at restaurants, and dark brown draperies made from outdoor fabric maximize year-round use of the space. Minimalist wood-and-steel tables and chairs finish off the dining space's elegant design.

The exterior's contemporary design extends to plant choices, mostly varying shades of green that provide welcome contrast to the home's neutral stucco tones and

wood-frame windows and doors. Old-growth redwoods on the back of the property shield several lounge chairs from unwanted views.

The space-conscious design of the home's exterior perfectly matches the interior, creating spaces that serve as extensions of the living area. It's an elegant, welcome, not-so-big solution.

A DRY-STACK FOUNTAIN IS THE STARTING POINT FOR THE FLOW OF WATER THROUGH THE YARD'S CHANNEL.

A SHALLOW CHANNEL FILLED WITH SMOOTH RIVER ROCK CUTS ACROSS THE LAWN AND UNDER THE PATIO.

COURTYARD VIEW

It started as a simple kitchen remodeling project, but when Susan and John Hoover realized they also wanted an outdoor spot in which to dine, the most natural place to look was the side yard—a barren 16×16-foot spot of dirt. "It was more convenient to have a patio in back, but that's far from the kitchen," Susan says.

Instead, when the couple flipped the kitchen around and added French doors, they enclosed the outdoor space, creating a charming, useful courtyard with a pleasing view. New, low brick walls topped with a loose-weave white lattice shield the area from street traffic but still provide a welcoming public view. A stylish green-painted gate, which matches the home's shutters, and white-painted arched arbor, fashioned out of four substantial 4×6 posts, lead out to the driveway.

The driveway's red brick border matches the low walls and complements the bluestone pavers in the courtyard. "Driveways can be really ugly, big expanses of paving, and ours goes right into the kitchen area and the entry door," Susan says. "That's what I see all the time, so I wanted [the driveway] to be a really nice, welcoming space."

Of course, the courtyard remains the main attraction, serving as a grown-up retreat and a spot for neighborhood kids to gather. "I tell them it's my playhouse," Susan says.

BLUESTONE PAVERS FILL THE PATIO FLOOR OF THE DINING SPOT, WHICH CATERS TO ALFRESCO MEALS OFF THE RENOVATED KITCHEN.

BY SCREENING THE COURTYARD FROM VIEW WITH OPEN LATTICE, THE HOOVERS GAINED A PRIVATE SPOT THAT'S FRIENDLY TO OUTSIDE VIEWS. A GATE COMPLEMENTS THE ARBOR AND LATTICE.

BRICK EDGES THE NEW DRIVEWAY, MATCHING THE LOW BRICK WALLS AND TYING EACH PIECE OF THE PROJECT TOGETHER.

5 AMENITIES

The key to transforming a basic outdoor space into an inviting retreat lies in the details. Early on, plan for an outdoor fireplace for warmth in the evenings, or an overhead fan to circulate cool air on hot days. Integrate built-in pieces including planter boxes for flowers or benches that double as storage space. Factor in water elements such as fountains and ponds. After construction is complete, the challenge lies in infusing your outdoor space with personal style. With so many options for outdoor furnishings, your choices range from classic wicker settees to sleek, contemporary loungers. Don't forget dining tables, end tables, and even sideboards for serving alfresco meals. Weather-resistant lamps and chandeliers ensure your time outdoors isn't limited to daylight hours. All-weather fabrics, artwork, and even sculptures help complete a personalized space that's sure to please.

Bringing Out the Best

It had good bones, but what Pam Chapman's exterior space lacked was clean-lined, streamlined style. So when she decided to redesign her Northern California home's interior spaces, it seemed only natural to extend the project to her outdoor living spaces as well.

"Including the backyard space in the home's interior design was natural," interior designer John Martin says. "The garden seeps into the house through a living room wall of windows and oversize French doors in the dining room. There was no differentiating the two."

The yard had the makings of a perfect space, with a wooded, secluded site and moderate climate. The backyard deck, surrounded by a lush canopy of foliage, made it ideal for outdoor living.

A relatively short list of existing items, including the 10×16-foot deck, several oak trees, and a few Japanese maples along the rear fence, remain from the original yard. The rest, the design team decided, was expendable. "The outdoor space was kind of a hodgepodge of a lot of different plants," Pam says. "I wanted a linear flow to it, a more modern look, and more continuity in the garden."

The new plants were selected based on texture and shape. Sporadic clumps of pink and yellow flowers, unhealthy plants, and overgrown ivy were replaced with mounds of mondograss, variegated lilyturf, shiny-leaf dwarf pittosporum, and Alaskan azaleas, for a lush, green, layered effect. "The space was quaint in size," Martin says, "and I wanted to streamline the plantings to match the simplicity of the home's interior."

In addition to careful plant selection, the structure of the space was carefully attended to as well. Deteriorating deck boards were replaced and stained, and a long bench added, spanning the side of the deck. The bench provides seating and disguises an adjacent retaining wall that was pushed back into the yard as far as the site's slope would allow.

Two steps down from the deck, a 10×15-foot slate patio doubles the usable outdoor living space. Its beautiful,

WHILE NOT ENCLOSED BY INTERIOR WALLS, THIS SLATE PATIO EXTENDS INDOOR LIVING SPACES OUTSIDE.

ELECTRIC, RETRACTABLE AWNING
SLATE PATIO
CONTEMPORARY FURNISHINGS

raw surface serves as an outdoor entertaining space and softens the outdoor area. An electric, retractable awning helps to shield guests from the elements.

Completing the indoor-outdoor transition, the exterior and interior are unified with accessories and furnishings. Several seating areas, filled with chunky, oversize, weatherproof furniture, transform the space into a true extension of Pam's interior living rooms. Well-chosen elements including floor lamps, metal sculpture, and outdoor cocktail tables finish off the space. "Sometimes it is not about redoing a space as much as it is bringing out its best," Martin says.

SEVERAL SEATING AREAS ALLOW PAM AMPLE ROOM TO ENTERTAIN, RELAX, AND ENJOY THE OUTDOORS.

THE CLEAN LINES AND SLEEK LOOK OF THE INTERIOR REDESIGN WERE EXTENDED INTO THE OUTDOOR SPACE TO ACHIEVE A MODERN VISION.

A CONTEMPORARY FOUNTAIN PERCHES ATOP POLISHED RIVER ROCK, ADDING THE SOOTHING SOUND OF RUNNING WATER TO THE OUTDOORS.

French Flair

Bill and Joanie Huck are the perfect mix for parties: He's a gifted cook, she's an accomplished hostess. But when they looked to their backyard, the couple knew it wasn't an adequate backdrop for their relaxed outdoor living and entertaining needs.

When the neighboring lot went on sale, the couple snatched it up. They added a detached garage and guesthouse, then crafted a welcoming patio and pool space to entertain parties from 6 to 60.

A TERRACE IN FRONT OF THE GUESTHOUSE AND GARAGE ADDITION SERVES AS A PRACTICAL OUTDOOR ENTERTAINING AREA.

A SEPARATE COOKING AREA KEEPS SMOKE AND ODORS AWAY FROM DINERS.

223

Architect Jim Kelley-Markham matched the exterior of the structure with the main home's Provençal style. Interior designer Caroline Murray helped ensure the exterior reconfiguration matched the home's interior without overpowering the scale of the backyard. Materials and architectural details including wood-shingled roofs, casement windows, and doors set in 12-inch-thick walls tie the addition with the terrace, garden, and pool.

A fireplace, the focus of the rear of the addition, fronts one section of the paved terrace, adding warmth to an intimate seating area. A simple arched trellis frames the built-in banquette and fireplace, while an overhead wire chandelier holds candles for a touch of romance. In a separate space, an outdoor grill, refrigerator, and sink provide a place to cook away from the main seating and entertaining areas. "At night in the summer, it actually gets cool here—50s and 60s—so the fireplace is a natural place to gather people," Joanie says.

A blonde mountain stone terrace runs behind the guesthouse, ending at the outdoor kitchen. Slabs of the same stones, which were sanded, form the raised edge platform of the 45-foot-long pool. "It's designed to be seat height so that it can also be a place for guests to sit and dine, like a long picnic table," Kelley-Markham says.

Spigots set in a stone wall turn the pool into a fountain. "We all felt the pool should be like an old French pond," Murray says. "The bottom should be dark, with slabs of stone going right up to the edge. When you turn on the water and hear it splashing, it's just like a fountain in Paris."

The Hucks and their children now use every inch of the backyard for entertaining, whether for an intimate gathering or entertaining large groups. It's French outdoor living at its best.

SPIGOTS SPOUTING OUT OF A TERRACE WALL IMITATE THE SIGHTS AND SOUNDS OF A PARIS FOUNTAIN.

A WIRE CHANDELIER LIT WITH CANDLES ADDS A ROMANTIC FLAIR TO THE DINING AREA. A FIREPLACE WARMS COOL EVENINGS, AND EASY-CARE FURNITURE ADDS TO THE LOW-MAINTENANCE LIFESTYLE.

Wall fountain
Bluestone patios and paths
Vine-covered, three-part pergola

Change brings opportunity and, for Babs Smith and Dan Sullivan, opportunity arrived in the form of an uninspiring backyard. After moving from Canada to Illinois, the couple realized that their new yard wasn't attractive, and didn't reflect their desire for a personal garden retreat. Remembering the lush, English-inspired gardens they had seen in Toronto, the couple imported a landscape architect from their native country and transformed the entire living space.

When landscaper architect Steven King arrived from Canada, he knew that the couple was seeking a garden sanctuary for personal solitude. "I try to create outdoor spaces that people can relax in when they are home," he says. Further, he understood that the formerly bland

Flowing over grand pergolas, pale-tone flowers form a comforting canopy for strolling and relaxation.

Transformed from an unimpressive yard, the new garden features an elegant combination of walkways, patios, and living spaces.

yard would have to be open and spacious enough for relaxed entertaining. "Babs and Dan are very much into entertaining outdoors, and the small space needed to seem larger and more interesting."

Basing his design on the American Georgian architecture of the couple's new house, King used every inch of the lot while maintaining harmony with the home. "The division of the outdoor rooms and spaces in both the front and back of the home needs to be appropriate to the architecture," he says. To match Georgian style, the garden exudes a British-tinged elegance mixed with a hint of European charm.

Exiting the house, a raised terrace serves as a primary gathering spot and faces an inviting fountain courtyard. Hiding the garage, a wall-size fountain set against a trellis establishes a blissful, welcoming atmosphere and draws guests to the space. Surrounding the courtyard on three sides, a grand, vine-laden pergola separates garden spaces and provides a comforting sense of structural

enclosure. With the flowing vines and flowers, the pergola creates distinct and alluring passageways from one garden area to another. Bluestone tiles form inviting walkways and patios around the yard, creating the impression of separate spaces. "The flow from room to room was designed to seem effortless," King says.

Running the length of the yard, from the side of the terrace to a corner nestled beside the garage, King created a secluded garden walkway. Near the patio, an unobtrusive herb garden invites visitors to stroll around separated planting beds. Following the bluestones to a

A RAISED TERRACE PROVIDES SPACE FOR DINING AND SMOOTHLY TRANSITIONS INTO THE CENTRAL COURTYARD.

A FOUNTAIN MADE FROM AN ANTIQUE FAUCET DISGUISES THE GARAGE AND PROVIDES A SOOTHING ATMOSPHERE FOR DINING.

hidden spot by the garage, a walkway circles a lava-stone birdbath and a ring of boxwood. Offering a place for peaceful reflection, this serene corner features a bench facing back toward the courtyard.

Even though the design has no grass lawn, a rich variety of foliage provides plenty of green scenery. "Color plays a very important part in our moods and I purposely designed this garden to be calming," King says. "I use plants that have great foliage, and the flower colors are limited to soft white, pale blue, violet, pink, and peach." Along with the enveloping privacy produced by the surrounding trees, the blending of light tones with the deep greens creates a soothing, peaceful effect. Using a variety of potted flowers allows the homeowners to change the type of plants or make particular effects mobile throughout the garden.

Long after the old, standard yard has been forgotten, Babs and Dan will have an unforgettable sanctuary. Lush and welcoming, the stone pathways lead through calming arbors and secluded old-world gardens. "The solitude of our garden is a treasured experience," Babs says. "It offers us our own oasis where we can not only enjoy the beauty of nature, but also the time we spend together."

A GRAND PERGOLA CROWNED BY WHITE ROSES CREATES AN ELEGANT FRAME FOR A DINING TERRACE AND A COURTYARD.

EVEN WITHOUT GRASS, A BACK GARDEN PROVIDES PLENTY OF COLOR AND VISUAL INTEREST BY USING FOLIAGE AND SCULPTURAL ELEMENTS.

AN AGED COPPER WEATHER VANE ADDS AN INTERESTING VISUAL ELEMENT TO THE COURTYARD FOLIAGE.

WITH A VARIETY OF FLOWERING PLANTS, THE PERGOLA SERVES AS A DIVIDER BETWEEN AREAS AND CREATES AN ENTICING PASSAGEWAY.

THREE IN ONE

If decks were dreams, then Karen Durham's included a small seating space off her bedroom to while away quiet moments. But dreams are often separate from reality—Karen and her husband Mike didn't know how to design that space or connect it to a larger eating area just 20 feet away. For that, they turned to local landscape designer Tina Nyce.

Nyce dismissed the idea of a single large deck. "If that entire area were a deck, it would be massive," Nyce says. "You would feel lost. It would only be appropriate for a huge party."

Nyce divided the space—which originally included a deck that barely held a table for four—into three intimate units without walls. She chose a variety of building materials and slight changes in elevation to mark distinctions in function. Two decks sit two steps above, and on either end of, a warm, gray sandstone patio. The decks, built of old-growth Western red cedar, run parallel to the house and contrast with the stone pattern. While there are no physical barriers, eyes and feet "tell you you're entering a different space," Nyce says.

The raised dining area off the kitchen has room for a wrought-iron table and chairs to seat six; surrounding

BUILT-IN PLANTER BOXES ADD TO THE FLORAL DISPLAY, CREATING AN ENVIRONMENT THAT'S COLORFUL AND RELAXING.

THE THREE "ROOMS" REPLACED AN ORIGINAL DECK THAT BARELY PROVIDED SPACE FOR A TABLE FOR FOUR. THE EXPANSIVE NEW DECK IS COZY AS WELL AS GENEROUSLY SIZED.

233

built-in benches provide ample room for overflow. On the stone tile patio, teak chairs surround a portable fire pit for roasting hot dogs or marshmallows.

The third area, Karen's dream space, is a small, sheltered seating area, accessible from the master bedroom through French doors. She and her husband relax there, surrounded by a trellis and arbor and screened from a neighbor's view by climbing roses . Fixtures here, too, play a key role; the chaise longues match the seating choices in the dining space, unifying the separate areas. Built-in planters filled with bursts of colorful flowers run right up to the house.

The multiple levels and strong lines of the space ensure that a small group feels cozy in one space, while a bigger group can also gather there comfortably.

TWO CHAISE LONGUES, SECLUDED BY A TRELLIS, SIT IN A SPACE JUST OFF THE MASTER BEDROOM.

TEAK CHAIRS SURROUND A PORTABLE FIRE PIT ON THE STONE PATIO. THE COUPLE'S TWO CHILDREN ENJOY THE BACKYARD PLAYHOUSE BUILT TO MIMIC THE HOME, COMPLETE WITH PORCH, GABLE, AND MAILBOX.

"I love the three different areas. Now we have room for a lot of people at dinner; I have a place to sit and read; and we can all relax on the patio, roasting hot dogs and marshmallows with the kids or enjoying a fire with friends," Karen says.

STONES CREATE A NATURAL PATHWAY THROUGH THE BACK YARD.

SEPARATE AREAS INCLUDE A SEATING SPACE AND A DINING AREA. THE CONTRAST IN MATERIALS AND HEIGHT DISTINGUISH DIFFERENT FUNCTIONS IN THE OUTDOOR RETREAT.

MOTHER NATURE DESIGNS

EVEN THE DINING TABLE, A HIGHLIGHT OF THE
OUTDOOR ROOM UNDER THE ARBOR, IS COVERED
WITH COLORFUL PLANTINGS.

STONE COLUMNS TOPPED BY LAMPS ENTICE THE
FAMILY TO USE THE PATIO LONG AFTER SUNDOWN.

A NEW LIVING AND PLAY SPACE KEEPS THE THREE
SMITH CHILDREN OUTSIDE IN THE AMPLE BACKYARD.

Prior to their backyard makeover, the Smith family
seldom ventured into their suburban home's backyard.
Now, Lil and Greg Smith and their three children are
drawn to the new outdoor rooms. Stone patios and paths,
a rustic arbor, a lush patch of lawn, and natural plantings shielded by the shade of mature pecan trees are too
tempting to resist. It's a complete transformation—the
backyard looks as if it was designed by Mother Nature.

"We wanted everything to look like it had been there
a while," Lil says, "so we were very selective of the
materials. We didn't want to introduce too many."

Landscape architect Elizabeth Smidt took a sensitive
approach in her design to achieve this goal. "The
property had a natural feel to begin with, and that feel
is what drove the design of everything we did,"
Smidt says.

The flowing paths and multiple tiers of curvaceous patios match the ample yard's hillside contours. This fluid design limits the size of the patios, which lead to small terrace spaces, so there aren't any large areas smothered by concrete.

The outdoor space is divided into an upper patio, a main patio with an arbor, the kids' patio, and a lower patio, each rounded in form. Fencing, arbor posts, trees, and shrubs suggest walls, while distressed cedar arbors form a ceiling. Pennsylvania multicolor flagstone in a mix of slate blue, purple, brown, rust, and buff is the perfect complement to the artificially aged arbor, which got its distressed look from sanders, wood burners, and heavy chains. Larger stones form the wider paths and the main 22-foot-diameter patio, while smaller stones on the narrow paths and intimate patios maintain the space's scale.

A rugged limestone with a pitted surface lends itself to the unrefined dry-stack look of the retaining wall, decorative columns, and base for the new grill. Lamps top the stone columns, transforming the yard into a comfortable, after-sundown spot during the scorching heat of Texas summers.

Today, visitors to the Smith's brand-new "old" yard comment on the mature, serene landscape, with nary a clue about the wholesale transformation that took place underneath the shade of mature pecan trees.

THE STONES OF THE GRILL BASE ARE MORTARED INTO PLACE, GIVING IT THE LOOK OF DRY-STACK.

FROM THE KITCHEN WINDOW, GREG AND LIL SMITH KEEP A WATCHFUL EYE ON THE SMALL-SCALE KIDS' PATIO WITH A PINT-SIZE TABLE, CHAIRS, AND BENCHES.

When Peter and Sonya Leonard moved into their Denver home, they weren't gardeners or deck builders. But they managed to substitute imagination for experience by envisioning an outdoor space perfect for relaxing, and eventually became their own small-space landscapers by putting pick axe to pavement themselves.

The tiny yard suffered from little character and even less charm. At 18×20 feet, the asphalt-paved space was no wider than a pair of parking spaces. To make matters worse, it was covered with a freestanding metal carport, and was open to an alley.

For starters, Peter pried up piles of paving along the yard's perimeter to create flower beds and a courtyard. The asphalt in the backyard's center served as the basis for a new patio, which was laid with bricks in an alternating pattern.

IN THE BACK, PETER CHIPPED OUT PAVEMENT ON THE EDGE TO ALLOW FOR FLOWER BEDS. THE CENTER PORTION SERVED AS THE BASIS FOR A BRICK PATIO.

THE ROOF OVERHANG SHELTERS A COMFORTABLE FRONT-YARD SEATING AREA. SOUNDS OF WATER FROM A SMALL POND HELP CAMOUFLAGE STREET NOISE.

A SMALL ITALIAN SCULPTURE IS CAREFULLY PLACED TO ADD INTEREST TO A SMALL RAISED BED.

The couple surrounded the area with a 6-foot concrete-block wall, which cuts the backyard off from the alley and turns the view inward. The stucco-coated wall is cloaked in vines of English ivy. An arched, rough-hewn door in the wall allows alley access. In the corner, a 6-foot apple tree shades a pint-size garden pool with a low stucco wall.

Along one wall of the house, Peter constructed a greenhouse by building up the soil behind the retaining wall that runs alongside the patio. The greenhouse's removable glass doors, fitted into frames above the retaining wall, provide protection in the winter and fresh air in the summer. "The greenhouse faces south, so it gets plenty of winter sunlight," Sonya says. "We grow herbs year-round in there."

The couple didn't stop their small-space renovation at the backyard, but applied their newfound knowledge to the 29×23-foot front yard too. A roof extension over the front patio, complete with sturdy, rough-hewn posts and beams, melds with the home's original architecture. The overhang adds shelter for a comfortable seating area, complete with all-weather cushions and attractive twig furniture. An expanded flagstone walkway links the

sitting area with a garden pond. A see-through, wrought-iron fence acts as a clear division between private space and the sidewalk, but still provides a welcoming view.

After gazing at the Leonard's front and back yards, no one would ever guess that their thumbs once lacked any shade of green.

BY EXTENDING THE ENTRY IN AN ARCHITECTURALLY CONSISTENT MANNER, THE COUPLE PROVIDED A SECLUDED SPOT FOR GATHERING AND RELAXING.

STONE STEPS LEAD TO A FRONT-YARD SEATING AREA, WHILE A ROW OF TREES ALONG THE FENCE ADDS PARTIAL PRIVACY.

SERENITY NOW

Hardworking, multifunctional spaces are an asset to any home, but a soothing retreat is just as important. The necessity of creating a space for rejuvenation and restoration was pivotal in the design of this unique San Diego balcony.

   "The goal was to give the space definition and a sense of privacy, without losing the view or feel of an outdoor room," interior designer Donna Hendrix says. While the

THE WROUGHT-IRON CHANDELIER IS THE CROWNING TOUCH ON THE BALCONY'S GAZEBO.

INTERIOR DESIGNER DONNA HENDRIX INTRODUCED ASIAN INFLUENCES TO THE BALCONY TO CREATE A RELAXING, REJUVENATING SPACE.

space uses its outdoor appeal, the added comforts of an interior room make the balcony a welcome escape. A sisal rug covering the floor like carpet possesses a tactile element to enhance the living space's design. The oversize furniture, constructed to withstand the weather, offers deep and inviting cushions.

CURTAINS FILL A CORNER OF THE BALCONY, MAKING IT FEEL LIKE ITS OWN ROOM.

THE TRADITIONAL STRIPED PATTERN OF THE CHAIR CUSHIONS IS OFFSET BY THE COLORFUL PURPLE THROW PILLOWS.

The space exudes a feeling of quiet beauty thanks in part to Asian-inspired elements. A Japanese water fountain emanates the soothing sounds of trickling water. Rich, eggplant-hue curtains accent the shades of green found in the cushions and surrounding trees. Shoots of bamboo and spiky grass grow in pots that rest on stools, end tables, and the balcony floor, further hinting at the space's Asian influences.

An arched, iron gazebo frames the open balcony, pulling the space together without detracting from its view of the city and San Diego Bay. The portieres hanging from the gazebo's frame provide the privacy of an indoor room's curtained windows. A wrought-iron chandelier hangs from the middle of the structure. In the evening, with the chandelier's candles lit, the space radiates a soft, glowing ambiance.

Some outdoor spaces require constant attention and maintenance, but this outdoor room was created to be enjoyed with minimal stress. Everything on the balcony is set—the furniture needn't be moved in and out depending on the weather, and the plants don't need weeding.

After a long day, this space is ideal for winding down. The combination of feng shui, Asian country furnishings, and subtle potted plants ensures a harmonious environment. Serenity truly is within reach.

CERAMIC POTS FULL OF GRASSES ARE ACCENTED BY BAMBOO AND OTHER NATURAL TEXTURES.

A SIMPLE TEAPOT SITTING ON A SIDE TABLE ADDS TO THE SERENITY OF THE PRIVATE BALCONY.

AN OVERSIZE CHAIR NESTLES IN THE CORNER, IDEAL FOR REJUVENATION.

Renewable Resource

For a deck to truly enhance a home, it needs to be more than a well-constructed accumulation of boards and rails. For these homeowners, their deck was perfectly acceptable in its basic structure. It possessed plenty of space for relaxing or entertaining and featured a broad set of stairs that encouraged movement into the yard. But it lacked the character that would make it an attractive asset rather than a mere add-on to the home.

The deck's makeover began at the most basic level. After a thorough cleaning with both hard bristle brushes and a powerwasher, the old, faded surface was ready to accept a new tone.

The platform and railings now feature a double-tone hue of natural cedar sealer and dark brown stain, a combination that matches the house's trim. The stain first provides the dark brown hue, then a cedar-tone wood protector adds an energetic sheen. The layers create a rich, vibrant appearance to the once worn-looking boards.

Rather than leaving the deck isolated and elevated away from the surrounding yard, a small, thoughtfully constructed garden blends the structure into its environment. Shrubs and perennials populate the beds along the sides of the deck, offering hardy, low-maintenance options. These resilient plants require little attention but provide color, foliage, and height, making the deck visually attractive and hiding the unremarkable sides. Wooden planter boxes line the railings, softening their caged appearance and providing a place for more heat-tolerant, flowering plants. Painted with the same stain and sealant layering, the planters are made of rot-resistant cedar and contribute a rustic charm to the spare deck.

To provide structure and a sense of definition, brick-paver edging outlines the garden. The garden soil is layered with mulch to set a clean, uniform appearance. While the edging and mulch create a visually appealing space, they also have practical gardening purposes. Edging prevents invasive plants from creeping into the

THOUGHTFUL LANDSCAPING AND CREATIVE ACCESSORIES TRANSFORM THIS FORMERLY SPARE, ISOLATED DECK INTO A VIBRANT DESTINATION POINT.

space, while mulch controls weeds and retains moisture during hot days. Complementing the pavers and the dark wood steps, limestone pavers extend into the grass and create an earthy entrance point.

Plant life creates a colorful and varied surrounding that makes the deck part of the yard, but accessories make the outdoor addition an attractive daily destination. Rather than the more common umbrella or awning, these homeowners opted to use a wall frame with curtains to provide shade when desired. Since the family

EVEN WHEN NOT IN FULL BLOOM, PLANTS OF VARIED HEIGHT AND FOLIAGE PROVIDE AN INTERESTING AND COLORFUL GARDEN FROM SPRING TO FALL.

LOW-MAINTENANCE PLANTS ON THE GROUND AND FLOWERING PLANTS ALONG THE TOP SOFTEN THE RAILING AND DECK EDGES.

spends most of its time on the deck during the late afternoon and early evening, the homeowners focus their shade needs entirely on the deck's west side. Useful both indoors and out, fabric shower curtains serve as a splendid deck accessory because they are durable, washable, mold resistant, and inexpensive. The curtains may be spread to provide shade and privacy or tied with a sash to create an attractive detail.

Having established a comfortable, private space, the final additions make the deck an inviting spot to sit and enjoy the atmosphere. Maximizing convenience and cost, plastic wickerwork furniture provides seating. The wicker style is unpretentious and charming, and the pieces are resilient against the elements and easy to clean.

Low maintenance and easy on the budget, this deck rejuvenation provides a vibrant connection between the house and the outside. Rather than an isolated addition to the backyard, the space now features a private, welcoming retreat that makes the backyard feel like part of the home.

WICKERWORK FURNITURE ADDS CHARM TO THE SPACE, WHILE ITS PLASTIC CONSTRUCTION ENDURES EXPOSURE TO THE ELEMENTS. PARTNERED WITH NEW CURTAINS FOR SHADE AND PRIVACY, THE RICH TWO-TONE DECK CREATES A REJUVENATED OUTDOOR RETREAT.

CEDAR PLANTERS MATCH THE DECK'S NEW COLOR TONES, RESIST ROTTING, AND ADD A RUSTIC TOUCH.

Architect Salvatore Balsamo and his son Tory already had urban sophistication in their classic Chicago graystone. But they wanted a touch of nature, along with some serene seclusion, in the middle of the big city. In an area where square footage is precious, Salvatore created an urban oasis by thinking upward rather than out.

While courtyard gardens may seem more suited to the tropics or New Orleans, Salvatore opened his living space to the fresh air by constructing an innovative, multilevel series of spaces that extend up three stories. "The whole idea was to create outdoor living spaces that we could use for family and entertaining in the summer," Salvatore says. The concept proves to be successful—the outdoor space now welcomes dining, office work, relaxation, and entertaining late into the evening.

The dramatic construction begins above the garage with a courtyard attached to the family room and kitchen. Blue slate tile dominates the floor while stucco painted a lively yellow provides a tropical freshness. Crown molding and a built-in bench create a sense of architectural definition.

A cantilevered fan hovers over the courtyard, moving air during warm weather, while a stucco-encased fireplace provides heat when the Windy City temperatures turn brisk. Combined with elegant copper wall lamps, a light in the ceiling fan offers a soft, enveloping glow in the evening.

"It's very comfortable," Salvatore says. "It's where we eat most of our meals in the summer. I wanted fun, lively, and upbeat colors and textures. With the yellow stucco walls, green-painted trim, and the slate floors, it feels like Acapulco or other tropical Mexican resorts."

Ascending a corkscrew staircase, a second open-air deck provides space for dining and conversation. Half of the deck offers white, wrought-iron seating and room to relax in the sun. The second half is a gated, private enclosure with cushioned wicker seating, lamps, and a television. Sheltered by the balcony above and connected to the home by French doors, the room is an outdoor refuge for solitude.

"The gated second level is off my study, and it's a place to read and have my morning coffee," Salvatore says. "I included the upper-deck seating areas to use for catered parties—the outdoor spaces, combined with the family room, have accommodated parties with 100 guests."

A balcony off Tory's room provides the final outdoor space in this layered marvel. Using vertical organization, Salvatore creates outdoor living that is both personal and shared by the family. Separated from the rest of the deck structure, the top deck offers individual privacy and a splendid view of old Chicago.

Creative design carves space out of a tight situation, but a profusion of plants brings natural color and serenity to an urban garden. Surrounded by an environment of concrete and asphalt, Salvatore uses a system of built-in planting boxes and mobile containers to create a vivid, growing garden in the center of the city. While the plants soften the urban edges of the graystone, sculptures, bird feeders, and wrought-iron gates add style and personality, building the sense of an old-world courtyard. Colorful annuals such as petunias mix with more exotic species, including palms and hibiscus. With plant life cascading from boxes and rising along trellises, the city dwellers welcome the lush, intimate refuge.

"When you're on the decks, you see the garden, not the buildings beyond," Salvatore says. "You're in the center of these flowers. There are also fragrances and the birds that visit our feeders know the garden better than I do. It's got the look, the sounds, and the smells of a garden. You don't feel like you're in the middle of the city."

A BAR-HEIGHT BISTRO SET SITUATED ON THE OPEN-AIR SECTION OF THE UPPER DECK ALLOWS SITTERS TO TAKE IN THE TROPICAL PARADISE.

THE FIREPLACE MANTEL, LINED WITH CANDLES AND POTTED PLANTS, ADDS TO THE OUTDOOR SPACE'S LIVING ROOM ATMOSPHERE.

Gardening requires dedication, but in such an unusual space it also inspires ingenuity. "When I first started these gardens, it would take me at least two and a half hours a day to water the plants," Salvatore recalls. Now a computer-controlled drip system provides necessary moisture without all of the legwork. "I set the timer and the amount of water needed, depending on what the weather has been like, and the irrigation system does the rest," he says.

With a flourishing garden nestled in a classic urban neighborhood, Salvatore and Tory enjoy the best of the city and country fused together. Privacy, solitude, and natural serenity make their multilevel deck an enticing destination day or night. Sitting by a fire, listening to a bubbling fountain, or simply admiring their garden, the fast-paced world of city streets seems far away. "The decks have really proven to be an extension of the house and have proven that you can do wonderful things in small spaces," Salvatore says.

AS LUSH GARDEN PLANTS CROWN THE COURTYARD, A FAN ON A CANTILEVERED BEAM COOLS THE SPACE DURING HOT CHICAGO DAYS.

FRENCH DOORS CONNECT THE INDOOR LIVING ROOM AND KITCHEN WITH THE COURTYARD OUTSIDE.

Sheltered by the balcony above and separated by wrought-iron gates, an outdoor room serves as a study for relaxing and reading.

Mirrors behind latticework create visual space and reflect sunlight as it descends into the courtyard.

Elegant wrought iron contributes to the deck's evocation of a serene country garden.

THE OPEN, SECOND-LEVEL DECK PROVIDES INTIMATE ENTERTAINING SPACE IN THE MIDDLE OF THE CROWDED CITY.

A LION'S-HEAD FOUNTAIN ADDS TO THE SERENE AMBIENCE OF THE GARDEN.

COPPER WALL LAMPS ADD RUSTIC, AGED CHARM AND SOFT, WARM ILLUMINATION.

NIGHT AND DAY

When the perfect evenings of a Midwestern summer beckoned, Jim and Dani Eldridge didn't want to abandon their patio and deck simply because the daylight had faded. Embracing an ambitious lighting project—from an open fire to lamps in the trees—the Illinois couple decided to expand their living room into the open air, and to extend their outdoor living late into the night.

With the assistance of lighting contractor Bob Hursthouse, the couple wanted to bring illumination to the darkness around their entire yard, providing light for both safety and design. If they were going to be strolling about the yard during night hours, and particularly if they were going to have guests, the Eldridges wanted safety to be a priority. Stone pathways and deck steps, while visually attractive, are precarious places when walking in the darkness. Although many yards have lights on poles, Hursthouse says these may be ineffective since they may cast long, deceptive shadows or shine directly into the eyes.

SOFTLY GLOWING LANTERNS PROVIDE A SOOTHING AND SAFE PASSAGE ALONG A WALKWAY.

WHEN DEVISING A LIGHTING PLAN, THE CONTRACTOR HIGHLIGHTED THE PATIO, GAZEBO, AND DECKS AS DISTINCT DESTINATIONS WITHIN THE SPACE.

A PRAIRIE-STYLE LANTERN PROVIDES STYLISH ILLUMINATION FOR AN EVENING STROLL.

The solution lies at stair-level. "If you put a light just above and behind the step so that it throws a shadow on the riser and the tread is illuminated, you see very clearly the light versus the dark and where to put your foot," Hursthouse suggests.

For more light, the Eldridges selected a low-wattage system that is easy to install and exercises a prudent level of precaution. If a wire is accidentally cut, the low wattage is relatively harmless, even if a child happens upon the break.

Safety may have been a first priority for the Eldridges, but their lighting system has the most dramatic influence on the outdoor space's appearance. Border lights accentuate the shape of an octagonal gazebo as recessed light shines upward into its rustic wooden beams. Once guests are drawn to the shelter, a dimmer determines whether the lighting is subdued or bright.

Nearby, underwater lights highlight a pond and water-fall, producing an entrancing glow. Even when the moon is not out, there's enough light for an evening stroll, thanks to lights mounted in the trees to enhance the natural nighttime glow. The lighting adds ambience to outdoor dining as well. "You can sit outside and see what you're eating without feeling you are under a spotlight," Hursthouse says.

Decorative details in lighting also create an inviting mood. Small Prairie-style, pagodalike lamps along the walkway provide a relaxed entrance to the home. Relying on a less technological light source, a round, open-pit fire serves as an irresistible centerpiece for the patio. Friends and guests may gather around the flickering illumination and enjoy quiet conversation late into the night.

For Hursthouse, lighting a backyard area must be thoughtful and flexible. Even when the Eldridges are away, a photo-cell timer turns illumination off at dawn and on at dusk, providing security as well as an alluring, golden presentation. Lighting conforms to the homeowners' mood with dimmers, while careful placement ensures an intriguing visual impact. "You don't want everything lit uniformly," Hursthouse says. "It takes away some of the charm."

For the Eldridge's outdoor living experience, the result is transformative. Whether bathed in sunlight, moonlight, or the new electric lights, their backyard welcomes and comforts guests anytime of day.

LIGHTS ON THE VERTICAL RISE LEADING TO THE GAZEBO ILLUMINATE THE STEPS FOR SAFETY, WHILE BORDER LIGHTS HIGHLIGHT THE GAZEBO AS A NIGHTTIME DESTINATION.

A CIRCULAR FIREPLACE DRAWS PEOPLE OUTSIDE FOR A RELAXING EVENING.

Pam and Steve Myrick knew they wanted to avoid slapping another standard 12×12-foot, pressure-treated pine deck next to their suburban home's obligatory concrete patio. Instead, the couple turned their pancake-flat, plain-Jane backyard into a space with character.

The 27×18-foot space is divided into one area for entertaining and dining, and another for cooking and relaxing. The deck, which is accessible from both the dining room and kitchen, is big enough to be hardworking, but small enough to be in proportion to the yard.

Curves and angles add visual interest in the square spaces, while the elevated structure defeats flatness and provides contrast. Deck boards set at angles enlarge the sense of space. The soft lines are functional as well. A curved rail surrounds a cantilevered bench, and a built-in flower box serves as another rail. Wide, wrap-around steps lead to a rock-filled bed, which acts as a transition between the contours of the structure and the green lawn.

The deck is constructed of ipe, a Brazilian hardwood. Although it costs slightly more than high-end redwood, it needs next-to-no maintenance and is extremely durable and termite-hardy. Ipe is so hard it doesn't accept nails; each hole must be predrilled, and stainless-steel screws serve as fasteners. Because ipe weathers to an ash gray, the Myricks stained and water-sealed the deck to retain its rich color.

The deck more than serves its purpose, and draws the couple outside often. "We've entertained more this year than in all the last five years," Steve says.

THE CURVED RAIL WRAPS A CANTILEVERED BENCH AROUND THE DECK, CREATING A PLEASING ADDITION TO THE RECTANGULAR BACKYARD.

A BUILT-IN FLOWER BOX SERVES AS A RAIL AND PROVIDES A COLORFUL BACKDROP FOR SEATING.

A STAINLESS-STEEL GRILL SET INTO BRICK CREATES A FOCAL POINT OF THE COOKING AND DINING SPACE.

TWO SPOTS OUTSIDE THE KITCHEN AND DINING ROOMS ALLOW FOR A WEALTH OF OUTDOOR LIVING, FROM COOKING TO RELAXING.

Happy Compromise

PAINTED BROWN TO MATCH DETAILS ON THE HOUSE, THE RAILINGS SERVE AS A POWERFUL ELEMENT CONNECTING DECK WITH HOME.

BRICK-AND-STUCCO PLANTERS MAKE THIS DECK SEEM LIKE PART OF THE HOME'S ORIGINAL DESIGN.

After Cathy Filgas and Shoaib Tareen expanded their Tudor home, the last thing they wanted was a stereotypical wooden deck. "I wanted something made with concrete," Cathy admits, "but our slope was too steep." The homeowners wanted outdoor access that wouldn't conflict with the style of their house, which is nestled beside acres of wetland. With the assistance of landscape architect Jane Duncombe and deck builder John Breiling, the couple found a worthy compromise, blending their home into a functional outdoor space.

Built-in kick-off mat

Brick-and-stucco planters

Moveable benches

The new deck provides a graceful transition to the timber in back while offering plenty of space for entertainment.

Built-in benches provide plenty of seating for entertaining. The benches' linear slats quickly disperse rain.

Stucco planters capped by bricks serve as gardening space in the deck and merge the area with the home's exterior.

Built of Western clear cedar, the wide, clean-lined, two-level deck spans almost the entire length of the house and is combined with material borrowed from the home's architecture. Stucco planters capped with brick echo the home's exterior and frame the deck, creating a sense of stylistic continuity.

To maintain a clean, unobtrusive presentation, the deck is constructed with clips and exterior sublevel adhesive rather than nails. The smooth surface provides an unmarked and uninterrupted finish, and with no nails penetrating the boards, moisture can't seep in and damage the wood.

Providing an unusual and attractive convenience, built-in, kick-off mats are set into the deck at the French door entrance, allowing occupants to stomp off debris from a hike in the timber. Although functional, the feature is also visually appealing. "The deck is long and wide," Breiling says, "and the mats help break it up."

To create a flexible space, Breiling designed and constructed benches that reflect the spare, linear style. Two L-shape benches on the lower level are built-in, while benches on the top level fit against the railings but are moveable to meet a variety of seating needs. "We

entertain a lot, so we needed a bench system to supplement our deck furniture and accommodate more people," Cathy says.

The final elements fusing the home with the deck are the railings. Rather than duplicating the platform stain, the railings feature a dark brown paint that coordinates with the cedar deck and matches the home's Tudor details. "A railing can define a space," notes Breiling. "This railing makes a strong statement."

With an open, sophisticated space that is tailored to their home and lifestyle, Cathy is pleased with the deck. "We're outdoors from May until October," she says. "We fling open the French doors in the morning and don't close them until the sun goes down."

IN PRACTICAL TERMS, THE BUILT-IN KICK-OFF MAT ALLOWS DIRT AND DEBRIS TO FALL BENEATH. IT ALSO BREAKS UP THE BROAD EXPANSE OF DECK.

BUILT AROUND AN ESTABLISHED FIR TREE, AN L-SHAPE BENCH CONTRIBUTES TO THE STRUCTURE'S CLEAN, ANGULAR SENSIBILITY.

HILLTOP RETREAT

The new, 2,200-square-foot hilltop deck in the back of Colleen and Steve McNally's San Diego home combines the best of interior comforts with Mother Nature's loveliness by incorporating built-in seating, an outdoor kitchen, and a fireplace across separate levels.

The addition transformed the ever-muddy yard behind the McNally's home into a useful, comfortable, and beautiful space. "They wanted to increase the use of the backyard not only for parties but also to spend time with their kids," outdoor kitchen designer Kristen Victor says. "When the weather's nice, everyone can sit outside and eat. It becomes a lifestyle."

Instead of the standard, flat structure, this deck adds angles and curves. A grand staircase combines two awkward stairways, connecting the home's main rooms to a redwood deck a story below. Distinct zones provide spots for entertaining, relaxing, playing, and dining, as well as areas for ocean viewing.

Tucked in a natural nook beneath the deck's winding staircase, the outdoor kitchen and fireplace act as the core of the space. A stainless-steel refrigerator, sink, and grill set on a slate patio provide plenty of appliances suitable for outdoor meals. Cozy, electric heaters warm the dining nook on cool nights. Weather-resistant materials such as metal framing, exterior stucco, and slate countertops withstand the salty sea air and mid-morning fog. "A deck can be nice-looking and aesthetically pleasing but still be durable," Victor says.

On the deck, built-in planter boxes and benches allow enough space for a variety of activities, from playing cards to hanging out under the stars. A railing serves as a safety element, while mounted stair lights prevent stumbles. Guests sit and relax, hang out in the kitchen,

A GRAND STAIRCASE LEADS TO A REDWOOD DECK AND SLATE PATIO. THERE'S ENOUGH SPACE FOR THE COUPLE'S THREE CHILDREN TO PLAY AND FOR ADULTS TO COOK DINNER.

281

or mingle on the heated patio space. "I could not hold the parties I do without the deck," Colleen says. "I feel like our house is bigger now."

The deck and patio offer plenty of safe spaces for the couple's three children to run and play. "I wanted to make sure there was nothing the kids could break," Colleen says. "Kids will be kids, and I wanted an area where we could be comfortable hosting their Cub Scout parties."

Now the family spends all of its free time throughout the week in their extended outdoor living space. "It's so convenient," Colleen says. "Everyone stays outside—and together."

THE COZY KITCHEN AND DINING NOOK, TUCKED UNDER THE STAIRS, IS THE PERFECT SPOT FOR ENJOYING THE CALIFORNIA WEATHER.

WROUGHT-IRON FRONTS, SLATE COUNTERTOPS, AND STAINLESS-STEEL APPLIANCES WITHSTAND THE SEA SALT AND MORNING FOG.

FABRICATED WROUGHT-IRON GRATES COVER THE
CURVED FIREPLACE. THE WEATHER-RESISTANT TILES
FEATURE A FLOWER DESIGN THAT MATCHES THE
WROUGHT-IRON CURLICUE ACCENTS ATTACHED TO
THE SIDES OF THE FIREPLACE.

THE GENEROUS SPACE, SURROUNDED BY SOFT
COLORS, IS THE PERFECT SPOT FOR OCEAN VIEWING.
ITS HILLTOP PERCH ACTS AS A PSEUDO TREEHOUSE.

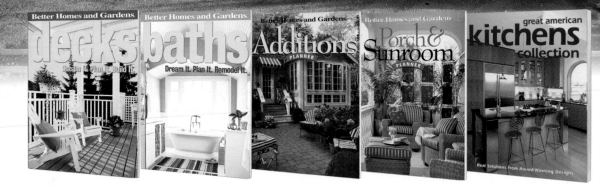